This is a must read: jam-packed with  in actual, lived experience. Entrepren and involves misadventures along the way. tackle misadventures head-on, develop practical solutions to any challenges that arise and learn how to embrace the uncertainty of not knowing what's going to happen next. (That's kind of the point of being an entrepreneur – to create a future that doesn't exist yet.) I would recommend this to anyone keen to learn what it really takes to be a successful entrepreneur. It's more attainable than you think.

**Jenny Britton – Head of Executive Development,
University of Edinburgh**

Having read many business books I can say that this has been by far one of the most relatable entrepreneurial books that I've ever had the privilege of reading. It delightfully presents the realities of being an entrepreneur including all the ups, downs and everything in between whilst providing an upbeat and practical guide for navigating the often bumpy road of being an entrepreneur.

The book has left me with an even greater sense of optimism and excitement for the journey ahead as I seek to apply the powerful lessons from within this book.

Dan J. Gregory – Founder, Elevate Media

I read *Misadventures in Entrepreneuring* in a few days. It was refreshing to hear a new perspective among a ton of other books professing to show you "the right way" to run your own business. Packed with self-reflection exercises, tips on how to course-correct and excerpts from interviews with entrepreneurs we can actually relate to (rather than the 1% of entrepreneurs who can relate to Richard Branson and Mark Zuckerberg), I found the book a great tool for helping entrepreneurs make entrepreneuring work for them. Whether you are looking for a bit of inspiration when you are feeling a bit stuck, or for a way to achieve more balance in how you juggle the 5,000 priorities in your life, this book will have something useful for you to take away and try out.

Sonia Codreanu – PhD researcher, University College London

Misadventures in Entrepreneuring is a refreshingly honest and raw journey through the emotional ups and downs of setting up and running your own business, no matter what the size and ambition.

Dan Moore – Studio Output

I LOVED this book! It's so refreshing to read an HONEST, BS and machismo-free first-hand account of what it's actually like to set up, run and exit a business. Anyone who wants to know what it's REALLY like running their own business should read this book.

Victoria Green – Victoria Green Ltd

Can I be totally honest? Truthfully I thought it was going to be very much like all the other entrepreneurial and start up books that have been written, but it's not!!!! It's about people, from different back grounds and in different careers (not all about how Deliveroo started on a shoe string and now a global multi-billion dollar company). It is about real people, real experiences, how they coped through difficult situations, their determination and drive and how you identify certain types of people which we can all relate too and how you genuinely care and want to help, rather than dictate on how we should run our businesses. It's talking our language! I LOVE IT!

Zoe Whittaker – Zoe Whittaker Ltd

THE TRUTH ABOUT HOW IT FEELS TO RUN YOUR OWN BUSINESS

BY GAYLE MANN & LUCY-ROSE WALKER

First published in Great Britain by Practical Inspiration Publishing, 2020

ISBN   978-1-78860-163-4 (print)
   978-1-78860-162-7 (epub)
   978-1-78860-161-0 (mobi)

Practical Inspiration
PUBLISHING

MIX
Paper from
responsible sources
FSC® C013604

TABLE OF CONTENTS

Why *Misadventures in Entrepreneuring* is the antidote to most business books you might have picked up before and why it's for you.

Trying to follow someone else's road map and getting nowhere, and why it's OK to feel like you're winging it.

So, you're doing it your way – but who actually are *you*?

A cautionary tale about passion; is it good and bad, and can you ever have too much of it?

Are you searching for work/life balance or are you actually desperately seeking a world where you feel less guilty about how you spend your time?

What happens when you're torn between something you love, and something else you love?

How to choose the people that will lift you up and how to spot the ones that won't.

Recognizing when you are successfully jeopardizing your own progress by allowing unexpected changes to stop you in your tracks.

DOMS, mental trips to the gym and other ways to get yourself unstuck quicker and dance jubilantly round obstacles.

What about life after this chapter of entrepreneuring? Who tells you when to move on or how it will feel? And what on earth happens next?

Where we're up to now and how we can still help!

NEVER-ENDING GRATITUDE

To the entrepreneurs who wrote this story with us – Paul Adams, Dan J. Astin-Gregory, Mandy Bailey, Emma Baylin, Mel Bound, Gary Butterfield, Antonis Chatzis, Lex Deak, Gillian Dick, Nick Elston, Chris Goodfellow, Victoria Green, Kerry Harrison, Roz Hutchings, Luke Johnson, Matt Kandela, Chris Lamontagne, Jim Law, John Loveday, Julie McGann, Gary Maitles, Lynn Mann, Daniel Marcos, Dan Moore, Scott Newby, Emily Newstead, Yekemi Otaru, Kate Percy, Stephanie Robinson, Chris Rooney, Mike Rucker Ph.D., Leah Steele, Diane Teo, Paul Thomas, Ben Treleaven, Lauren Valler, Anna Ward, Lynn White – you were brave enough to speak out so that others could benefit.

To the courageous entrepreneurs that we have been through thick and thin with and who are etched on our hearts and will always be at the heart of everything we do.

To our families who have always supported us no matter what – Linda, Rob, Al, Jordan, Jim, Hannah, Laura, Elspeth, Mike, Ruari, Moira, Barbara, Marina, David, aunties, uncles, cousins, great aunties and uncles and a whole bunch of those second mums, sons and daughters, brothers and sisters and aunties and uncles that belong to other people but you just adopted us as your own.

To our friends who think we're a bit mad but love what we do and the joy it brings us even if they don't know what the f**k it actually is. We've laughed and cried with you and we could not do this without the catharsis that only friends can bring. You know who you all are.

To the many coaches, mentors and professionals who have guided and championed us throughout this whole adventure. So many but a few who were particularly special to us – Ken Barclay, Martin Darroch, Jo Grant, Alan McColm, Mark McFall, Brian McGuire, Danielle McLeod, the team at NatWest, Ram Ramakrishnan, Craig Reid, David Reynolds, Alison Rose, Paula Skinner, Laura Sutherland.

To the Entrepreneurial Spark team past and present – you are the most incredible bunch of Go Do'ers with whom we had the privilege to work alongside. In particular, Jeremy Ambrose, Mike Stephens, Joe Trodden, Ria Tucker and Fay Watkin, still walking the walk every day.

To the team at Practical Inspiration Publishing and especially Alison Jones. And to those that helped us actually commit words to paper – Ginny Carter for always encouraging us to be ourselves and Karen McArdle for whom I (Gayle) will always be grateful for telling me my writing was self-indulgent. 😊

And finally, to Mika and Belle for your unconditional four-legged devotion…

We are grateful to every one of you.

WHY ARE WE HERE?

Here's the good news. Our first promise to you is that this isn't going to be one of those, *we started small, we grew huge, we exited and now we're penning our memoirs about all the things we did right after the event to inspire you to do the same,* type of books. If that's what you are looking for, then there are plenty more out there to choose from. In fact, this book is quite the opposite.

Misadventures in Entrepreneuring is designed to be the antidote to most business books you might have picked up before. This is not a glamorized or romanticized version of the truth about entrepreneuring; it's an identifiable collection of stories told by entirely ordinary seeming, but highly relatable people and how they do amazing things. These aren't aspirational stories being told from our millionaire mansions or our private islands. Not yet anyway. This aspirational story is coming to you from a spare bedroom home office on the banks of a canal, in Glasgow, and you don't get much more optimistic than that.

What's compelled us to be so honest about our experience, and as it turns out, the experience of thousands of other entrepreneurs we've met, is that for many reasons most entrepreneurs are afraid to fully open up about what it's like to *be* an entrepreneur. And we don't mean how to run a business, but the truth about how it feels to walk a day in your shoes and what you'll unexpectedly discover along the way. Truth – we've unexpectedly learned more in the last eight years than either of us did in the years before being part of our start-up. Like, a shedload more. And not just about business: mostly about ourselves, being entrepreneurs and being human.

No one tells you that's what is going to happen when you start a business. Yes, we all know that being an entrepreneur is about more than just figuring out how to run a business. But no one really talks about the exponential personal development learning curve to rival the summit up Mount Everest. Or about the learning to get comfortable with being excruciatingly uncomfortable side. Or how it's going to flip your brain upside down and inside out. Or how you'll experience an orchestra of emotions on a daily basis. Or, as one of the entrepreneurs we interviewed describes it: 'I wouldn't describe myself as a manic depressive... but I regularly swing wildly from manic to depressive and everything in between.'

The thing that really gets us is, even if some of the been-there-done-that stories do touch on the psychological side of being an entrepreneur, no one tells you that it's 100% normal to feel the way you do on any given day. Yes, even the days when you cannot imagine another person on earth could ever feel what you're feeling right now.

So, we felt it was our duty to share. To share inspiration *and* information to help you to respond to all of that unknowingness and aloneness. The sort of stuff we wished we'd known, and the things that other people don't talk about. We want you to know that you are normal and not a manic, or a depressive, or an alien with your head screwed on backwards. And that you're not doing it all wrong... at least not all of the time anyway. And we want to show you how to do it in a way that is going to feel much more like your way.

Warning to all: This book contains feelings.

Misadventures in Entrepreneuring is not just our experience but one voice telling the collective stories of everyone we've encountered along the way. There'll be no sugar-coating and no filters. You'll learn about our gin habit and a time we call 'The Fat Years', you'll hear stories from others including the day that entrepreneur Mel had to make an owl-shaped birthday cake with her daughter when she should have been writing her investment pitch because, well, life happens.

And you'll learn about your way of entrepreneuring, the way that is fantastically unique to you. How you can be your own best friend in business but, ironically, how you can also misadventure by being the only person throwing up walls to block your progress. How you can wrap yourself up in knots and thinking patterns, and what those damn feelings can do to you. How they can be really helpful but also very flipping unhelpful!

These are all things we learned the hard way, but then we realized that there isn't actually any other way when it comes to doing hard things – the hard way *is* the way. But we'd like to make it *less* hard for you if that's at all possible, or at the very least let you know what to expect, and help you figure out how to overcome your hard things.

This means giving you information, new ways to think, things to try and ways to avoid or minimize misadventuring. By the time you finish reading, we promise we'll have given you the tools to explore and exploit your own unique version of what it means to be an entrepreneur – to do things your way, on your own terms and to be in control of building the kind of life you really dreamt of when you set out.

We've designed each chapter to send you on your way to master a specific element of thinking and acting like an entrepreneur. We do this by giving you practical tools to use and show you how to put them into action in different ways. We'll show you how we did it, but we'll also show you multiple alternatives from other relatable entrepreneurs so that you can find a way that fits you best.

In every chapter we'll talk about how you can learn to course correct yourself if you feel you're going off track and we'll give you helpful bonus exercises to do. At times it's going to feel hard and your brain is going to hurt, but we promise you the results will be worth it. Lastly, because we know that time is the only thing you cannot get back, and there is no better time to do the hard things than now – at the end of each chapter we'll give you suggestions for helpful things that you can try right away to keep you progressing in the right direction. Things to *Stop* doing, things to *Start* doing and things to *Continue* doing.

To make sure these are always in your mind we've printed a whole page with these words on it and we've purposely kept the other side blank so you can tear it out, or cut it with scissors if the whole idea of tearing an actual page out of an actual book freaks you out.

But go on. Do it now! And stick it somewhere you can see it daily.

STOP...
START...
CONTINUE...

Why should you trust us? To start with, we both have a lengthy background in start-up. Lucy-Rose has been involved in a long list of start-ups, all with a Scottish streak. From launching a 'tartan affinity' credit card with a US bank aimed at the Scottish diaspora, she moved on to promoting her own board game, *Scottish Quest*. She also has a degree in Psychology and is a qualified business coach, so she definitely gets how people tick. I have a degree in Entrepreneurship and have worked in start-up for my whole career. From technology and investment, to tourism, franchising, innovation and invention I have had a 19-year love affair with entrepreneurs in the UK, Latin America, Eastern Europe and the Middle East.

We put all of that experience to the test over a period of eight years, starting in 2011, when we grew Entrepreneurial Spark – The World's Largest Fully Funded Entrepreneurial Accelerator. In short, a physical place that removed all the physical barriers to starting a business, like access to professional office space and IT, leaving us to support the empowerment of entrepreneurs to overcome the psychological barriers to start, grow and scale a business.

Originating in Scotland, we saw that the market for supporting start-up businesses was ripe for disruption. Dominated by public sector organizations who prided themselves on doing things the way they'd always been done, this left a gap for a new player in the market to reimagine what actually worked for entrepreneurs.

Where the traditional model of business support focused on the business itself – from business planning, to financial forecasts and product development, and all of the other necessary business bureaucracy – Entrepreneurial Spark took a different approach. We focused on the people and enabling the entrepreneurial mindset and entrepreneurial behaviours of the founders. And we did this on the basis that as an entrepreneur you can have the best business idea in the world, but it doesn't matter if you (the human) aren't able to execute on the idea effectively and keep getting in your own way.

We worked hard on the approach, starting with 35 entrepreneurs and enabling them for over a year to really home in on how they thought and acted. We then expanded to three locations in Scotland. Fast forward to the end of 2017 and we had 13 locations in the UK, two in India, 40 staff, and we'd worked with over 4,000 entrepreneurs.

We promised this wasn't a start small/grow big rags-to-riches tale at the start of the book and we're sticking to that promise. But we wanted to give you the assurance that we've observed, laughed, cried, worked and celebrated with, and most importantly learned from, over 4,000 wonderfully different entrepreneurs.

This isn't just our story, but a collection of stories, hints, tips and coping strategies from everyone we've worked with, as well as a bunch we've just met while we hunted for stories. This book draws on our own collective experience and knowledge but is penned by me, Gayle, from both of our perspectives. We believe this is your story too – maybe not yet, or maybe it's been your story for a while and you're looking for someone to empower you to do something even greater. We are lucky and we have had each other but we know that entrepreneuring can be lonely. We don't believe we could have done it alone and we don't want you to have to either.

What we've learned over the last eight years is that (and we don't mean this to sound cringey) we are people-people. We care far less now about the number of entrepreneurs we work with, and care way more about the human beings behind the businesses: you are incredible individuals.

Success for us is not how many books we can sell or how many lives we can impact, but the impact we can have on one person's life – maybe yours. If we can help you to nurture who you really are as an entrepreneur and encourage you to stop, start or carry on pursuing whatever you're doing now so you can build that life for yourself that feels more fulfilling than you ever imagined, then we'll have fulfilled our purpose.

The fact that you are still reading tells us that you want this in your life. Having some real entrepreneur friends and role models to look to is just the tonic you need to drive you forward. You already know the five things that Bill Gates does before breakfast or the habits of highly effective people, but yet they don't quite fit with the way you do things. By starting this book today you'll find many personalities and real role models inside these pages that we think you'll relate to, as well as the practical guidance, inspiration and motivation to be more adventurous than you ever previously dared to be.

Adventure awaits, let's get going…

1

Misadventures in...

ENTREPRENEURING

Let's talk about misadventures

When we began telling people that we were going to call our podcast and our book *Misadventures in Entrepreneuring*, the reaction we got from almost everyone was almost identical. It goes a little like this:

Them:	*What are you up to now you're not doing Entrepreneurial Spark any more?*
Us:	*We're writing a book! And launching a podcast!*
Them:	*Oh that's cool. What's it about?*
Us:	*Well, it's called Misadventures in Entrepreneuring and it's about…*
Them:	*[knowing smile] [chuckle]*
Them:	*Oh, I could tell you a few stories/I've certainly had a few of them myself…*

(Repeat for everyone we met.)

The funny thing about using the word *misadventures* and the reason we believe that everyone is familiar with it is that deep down we *all* know that the road to success is not a straight line or quite as simple as putting one foot in front of the other. We *all* know that it's going to be challenging and it's going to test us in ways we've never been tested before. Yet… we remain optimists. So much so in fact that we *all* (yes, you too) hope that we might just be the exception to the rule. And we remain optimistic, and steadfast in our resolve, that although all the evidence points to the contrary, we have got it sussed and we are not going to be the ones to veer off track. Until we do. And despite all of our best efforts, our positive thinking, our painstaking planning, and all of the books we've read about how others have become successful – we find ourselves (through no apparent fault of our own) in the midst of a place that we never expected to be. A challenge, or as we like to call it, a *misadventure*.

Sound familiar?

If it does, and you are one of those that are giving a knowing smile at the page right now and thinking those exact 'oh yup, that's me' words, then you are in the right place. You're part of our gang. Because we've all been there and we all have misadventures, yet no one talks about them. Which we think is weird and really unhelpful so we're going to. Firstly, because misadventure is a much more forgiving word than failure and in fact we're not talking about failure because despite the consequences of the misadventure, there will be a way back. And wouldn't it be nice to celebrate the idea that we tried something and it didn't quite turn out the way we thought, instead of considering it a failure?

Secondly, we want to talk about it because we would have found it really helpful to know we weren't alone in trying to find our way. We also love talking to people about their misadventures because it makes us feel infinitely better about ourselves and our own misadventures.

Thirdly, we're on a bit of a rant about all the unrelatable so-called *advice* doing laps around social media about what it's like to be an entrepreneur, and we are struggling to keep our mouths shut so we really wanted to hear from some more relatable role models.

And finally, we want help! We wanted to hear what other people do when they find themselves having a misadventure. Does everyone drink gin, or eat their body weight in tacos, or lock themselves in a room and lie on the floor hoping the misadventure will pass? We want to know! And we think you do too.

In writing this book and putting together the podcast, as well as our previous work with entrepreneurs, we've spoken to some amazing people. You've probably never heard of them before, but they make up a whole gang of unsung entrepreneuring heroes that make for way better role models than the ones we're used to seeing on *The Apprentice*. And it started to become apparent that there are some really common (and obvious with hindsight) reasons why we misadventure. They're all human nature, but like most things we're blind to them until they're right there in front of us or until someone else points them out.

In the coming chapters we've pulled together the ones we see most often in the hope it gives you a bit of a heads up when you are heading off down a rabbit hole in the future.

In this chapter we're going to introduce the biggies – the real misadventures. The things that, if you take nothing else away from the coming pages, you should remember these four principles.

1. The perception of being an entrepreneur is always different from the reality.
2. Misadventures aren't caused by the businesses; they're caused by the people running the business and the stories you're telling yourself.
3. Misadventures are also caused by trying to be someone else's version of an entrepreneur – be your own version.
4. You don't know what you don't know, that's OK; everyone else is winging it too.

The perception of being an entrepreneur is always different from the reality

Unless you have been living under a rock, you won't have failed to notice that the last 10 years has most definitely been the decade of the entrepreneur. With names like Jobs, Zuckerberg, Sandberg, Musk, Huffington and Besos becoming aspirational figures in home offices, co-working space and accelerators around the world, never has it been cooler or sexier to call yourself an entrepreneur.

But with this new wave of entrepreneurial role models has also come a slightly darker side of living the entrepreneurial dream – the media portrayal of what an entrepreneur should look like, how you should act, and the personal sacrifices that you have to make to be successful. I'm talking about the 'hustle', the 'grind', Gary V shouting at you from YouTube, endless memes of *The Wolf of Wall Street* winking at you over a champagne saucer, *The Apprentice* and other enormously unhelpful portrayals of an entrepreneur that are so far from reality that they're verging on negligent.

The problem with these perceptions is that, for people like you and I, they are hugely unrelatable. I don't know about you, but my home office doesn't have a Necker Island ocean view.

I've got to get my inspiration from the view of the housing estate playpark out of my spare bedroom window on a dismal October day in Glasgow.

In 2014, the US TV show *Silicon Valley* started to reverse this trend by ridiculing the tech industry start-up cult in the US, and Arianna Huffington is the latest high-profile entrepreneur to call time on hustle culture and urge us all to get a bit more sleep. Back in Glasgow, my co-founder Lucy-Rose Walker and I are on a mission to resolve this in our own way.

We witnessed entrepreneurs day in and day out revere the aforementioned role models, and perhaps we hero-worshipped them a bit ourselves, until eventually we all came to a place where we found the reality to be somewhat removed from the dream. On most days we found ourselves out of our depth, and our comfort zone, with no one to call on who could relate to or empathize with us... and social media was certainly no consolation.

It was tough and although we were extremely lucky that we had each other, we still felt pretty alone and anxious that we were winging it all the damn time. We longed for someone to tell us it was normal, OK even, and that they were going through something similar too. We hankered after someone to help us take some of our misadventures and some of the pickles we'd found ourselves in less seriously. Or to know that other people do their best work over a plate of scampi and chips and a very large, cold glass of sauvignon blanc. We craved some relatable role models. Then, we interviewed Victoria Green who gave us something we could finally relate to.

Victoria Green – Victoria Green Ltd

Entrepreneurs wear suits, entrepreneurs do this, entrepreneurs have posh cars, and programmes like The

Apprentice – they don't help. Oh, and entrepreneurs have to be massively good-looking! I just kept thinking this isn't normal… as I battled through the snow on my bike to a meeting – thinking I am a businesswoman; I shouldn't be riding a bike.

And actually, it was having the confidence that I was working in my spare room, and that was OK. I didn't have to pretend to be in an office somewhere. And it's OK to say if you don't know something, that actually no one expects you to know it all.

I think the problem is when you get an article in a magazine like the one I had, it's a great vehicle for the business, but what it does is create an unrealistic image of yourself that you're portraying to people. And even my friends say: 'You're doing really well, I saw you on LinkedIn and you're doing really well', and I'm thinking – 'Yeah, I'm doing really well… on LinkedIn!'

I'm not saying that we shouldn't admire the achievements of our favourite famous entrepreneurs. Of course we should. And we should definitely aspire to do really big impactful things and make our mark on the world like they have. It's just that the glamorized marketable memes on how to go about it aren't helpful when everyone's experience is so different.

Lucy-Rose and I set off on a mission to find more people like Victoria, people who were willing to tell the brutally honest truth about what it's like to be an entrepreneur on a daily basis – the reality, not the perception. And it turns out that they exist, and they're everywhere, and they love to have cathartic conversations about things like how you've got 99 problems and every one of them is a human. Or 'depending on the time of the day it is, you'll feel like starting your own business is either the greatest or the stupidest thing you'll ever do'. That one was from Matt Kandela, who opened up about how dangerous these unrealistic perceptions can be and the kind of things he wished others had told him.

Matt Kandela – Dear Future

I think the one thing that no one says is how hard it is. Entrepreneurship is actually quite a dangerous word in some ways because there is a mythology around it, the idea spawned by the likes of Google, Facebook and Apple – the businesses that were started in garages and became global powerhouses – has created this myth that anyone can become a great start-up founder and make hundreds of millions of dollars and all you need is a great idea.

It's dangerous because – it's so hard! The toughest time for me was last year when my wife was pregnant, and she was in hospital for a month before she gave birth. It was terrifying and you're trying to juggle being there as a husband, worrying about your wife, worrying about your unborn child and knowing that if you're not doing work then the business isn't moving forward. So, you're literally trying to eke out hours at crazy times of the day because there is no option. And that is quite a dramatic piece when you have something huge in your personal life, but no one ever tells you about that... and that's when you have those thoughts of 'is this the right thing?' because if it's not, have I wasted those years?

You definitely have to go into this with your eyes open.

Don't worry: you can still have that dream of building that global powerhouse from your garage or your spare bedroom, but just be aware that having a great idea and simply making it happen isn't the full story.

The biggest challenge we have had as entrepreneurs is between what is projected as the life of an entrepreneur in the media or on social media, and how we feel about it on a daily basis. It makes you start to question everything about it, about yourself and if you're 'doing it right'. We felt like we had a duty to bring you the kind of stories that would give you a much more transparent account of what it takes to get yourself there, and to make you feel less like no one quite gets where you are.

Misadventures aren't caused by the businesses; they're caused by the people running the business and the stories you're telling yourself

Let me explain. When Entrepreneurial Spark began, our sole purpose was to support entrepreneurs to start their businesses by removing what we thought were traditional barriers and blockers to start-up, like access to office space and professional meeting space, IT and infrastructure, and access to quality mentors. And while this absolutely worked to help overcome some of the initial challenges, it quickly became apparent that supporting entrepreneurs was way more complex than that.

Because, as we discovered, supporting entrepreneurs is far *less* about the technicalities of running the business and far *more* about you the individual and what happens every day inside your head. And despite the general catch-all term 'entrepreneur', used to describe someone who starts a business, entrepreneurs like you and I are anything but general or catch-all.

We're big Tony Robbins fans and we now know this is what we should have been focusing on:

> *The most painful mistake I see in first-time entrepreneurs is thinking that just having a business plan or a great*

concept is enough to guarantee success. It's not. **Business success is 80% psychology and 20% mechanics.** *And, frankly, most people's psychology is not meant for building a business.*[1]

Tony Robbins

We had fallen into our own trap and hadn't been putting the entrepreneur at the heart of what we were doing. And I mean *really* putting the human at the heart of it. We'd been trying to solve business problems like desk space and access to the internet and hadn't been trying to solve mindset problems. Like doing things for money not because you love them, or being too afraid to speak to customers in case you don't like what they tell you, or not being accountable for your actions.

These are the real problems that entrepreneurs face. Not fretting about whether or not we've invented the world's latest and greatest gadget or widget, or whether we know how to write business plans or build financial forecasts, but whether or not the stuff that goes on between our ears every day is really fit for building our business.

If you don't believe me then think back to the last time you were stuck in your business, like really stuck. Or found yourself in a situation you never thought you could reverse out of. How did you get unstuck? How did you move forward? Be really honest with yourself. Did the situation change, or did you change your approach to the situation? Were you able to see it from another perspective? How did you get out of it? Sleep on it? Go for a run? Ask someone to help?

---

[1] Ryan Robinson (2020), '60 top entrepreneurs share best business advice and tips for success'. Available from: www.ryrob.com/start-business-advice/ [accessed February 2020].

Our thoughts and actions are the most powerful tools we have in our survival kit. Used properly and you could be unstoppable. Of course, we recognize that understanding the mechanics of building a great business has to come with the territory. But it's only the 20%, and you can also hire other people to teach you that bit. What will set us apart and what will make us truly great is harnessing our ability to think differently, to challenge the way we think, and the way others think, and to respond differently in the face of adversity.

But being able to challenge or change our thoughts is hard! You can't just wave a wand and it magically happens. You only get good at it with practice and lots of it, and it's about being brave enough to be honest about the kind of hard questions that we ask during the 'Course Correction' section of this book. This is your permission to be self-involved. Not in a navel-gazing way; this is not self-absorption. You only have permission to get involved with yourself to the point where you can look objectively at what you've been up to and do a really critical analysis of whether or not it's getting you to where you want to go.

The first and the most important course correction for you to learn is to accept that being a good entrepreneur is not about being good at business. It's entirely possible to be good at business and be a terrible entrepreneur if you don't have the right mindset. Being a good or a great entrepreneur is about embracing the fact that you are (almost) always both the problem and the solution to becoming great. This ship isn't steering itself; you are the captain and being a good entrepreneur is about choosing how to ride the waves.

Are you up for having a cold hard look at yourself?

Misadventures are also caused by trying to be someone else's version of an entrepreneur – be your own version

If you are a first-time entrepreneur, you could absolutely be forgiven for thinking that entrepreneurs are all alike. Like us you have probably read articles and books, been sucked into the hustle culture, watched videos, or even studied entrepreneurial characteristics and determined whether or not you fit the mould.

The real truth is that there is no mould. There is no mould because entrepreneurs are humans, and no two humans are alike. From the way we look and the way we dress, our hair colour, our skin colour and our DNA, right down to our childhoods, backgrounds, educations and life experiences, we are all a 100% unique combination of every technicolour moment we have been alive that no one can ever replicate.

Saying that every entrepreneur is alike is like saying that Barack Obama and Donald Trump are alike because they have been Presidents of the United States of America. Or Oprah and Ellen DeGeneres. Or because Van Gogh and Picasso are both artists they behave in the same way. I could go on, but aside from picking up a paintbrush every day (and an apparent artistic madness perhaps) we could probably agree that's where the similarities end.

Being an entrepreneur is simply the profession that you have chosen. Yes, most entrepreneurs will have shared experiences, and yes you will come across similar challenges or misadventures even. But you will also make your own decisions and approach these in your own way.

Think of it as if you were your own brand of superhero: everyone has their own powers; everyone overcomes situations using their powers differently. It's the same with entrepreneurs – the end goal is the same but the way you go about it will be fundamentally different from everyone else. Which means that it doesn't matter how much you study how other people have walked this path before; it won't be the way that you walk it.

Becoming a great entrepreneur is not just about reading books about what other great entrepreneurs do and absorbing the information or copying their actions. It's about trying things out for yourself, making mistakes on your own terms and figuring out what works for you. If you really want to find your own path then step away from all of the articles, blog posts and social media feeds that tempt you into emulating the five things Bill Gates does before breakfast, or 'read these 10 books this year if you want to be successful'. Bill's blueprint will be helpful to a point, but only you can find your way to the end on your own.

So, if you ever find yourself off course and heading in the direction of misadventure, it's most likely because you're following someone else's road map or trying to be someone else, and not being brave enough to do the things that are right for your own set of circumstances. Yes, you can learn a lot about sprinting from watching someone like Usain Bolt perform, but he also won Olympic Gold after fuelling himself with a plate of chicken nuggets. It doesn't mean that same strategy will help you become a better sprinter. The crucial part of that process is to apply what you learned to your own individual entrepreneurial DNA and do it your way.

Victoria Green – Victoria Green Ltd

> *When I left the accelerator, I felt that I needed to get an office because that's what you do. I found it really difficult being full time in the office with a team. Sometimes I need to be at home in a room by myself. Then we saw a house*

that was big enough to have an office and I realized that I never wanted to have an office that was never the way I wanted it.

And then I had this realization that it is my business, I don't need an office and I can do what I want.

I think everyone thinks they should be doing this one amazing thing, but no one knows what it is. I've realized that it doesn't exist – there is no road map. I've gone off track a few times, like the office, but I think when you recognize it you can come back from it. You can make mistakes and come back from them and it's OK.

You're not immune to the approach of trying to find the entrepreneuring elixir: we do it all the time too. Then we have to remind ourselves to take what we've learned and figure out how to make it work for us.

Case in point: I recently bought Tim Ferris' book – *Tools for Titans*. If that isn't looking for a road map to follow, then I don't know what is. I admit it, I was looking for answers! And depending on how you look at it that was what I got – about 113 different answers.

Then I had my own epiphany and the realization that every one of the 113 'Titans' that were featured had one thing in common – they weren't instantly famous, or good, or rich or successful, they just experimented to find the key things that worked for them individually and then they practised every day. There was no single success recipe for them, and they all created their own road map for success.

There are a few notable exceptions of things that virtually everyone does, like daily yoga or meditation and getting enough quality sleep, but other than that each person's path to becoming a titan in their field was entirely unique to the next.

This means that the buck really does stop with you and me. The hardest work you and I will do as entrepreneurs will be on ourselves. Ideally, you'll have done a bit of this before you take your first step as an entrepreneur, but if you haven't, then the next best time to start is today.

Some of you will find this prospect terrifying and some of you will find it exhilarating, and some will find it way too much like hard work – but what an opportunity to create a business and a life that is entirely bespoke to you. A life that you are totally in control of and responsible for, and one that will ultimately take you in the direction of your dreams and goals.

Although this book doesn't contain a magical map or a silver bullet, luckily for you it is chock-full of things you can do and hard questions to ask yourself to make sure you are heading in the right direction. It should also prevent unnecessary misadventures.

The first thing you need to do is figure out who you are and what you want, which can be harder than you think! When Lucy-Rose became CEO of Entrepreneurial Spark she had never been a CEO before so did what is natural to all of us and looked to others to find out who a CEO 'should be'. She was shocked to find that by and large the perception of the world was that CEOs were extroverts, that they were charismatic leaders, and her personal favourite – they have balls (not literally). It was so daunting and uncomfortable for her, especially as an introvert.

She eventually found her rhythm through working with a trusted mentor who helped her to figure out who she was and what she really wanted and then apply that to becoming her own version of a CEO. It wasn't an easy process though and it wasn't without a period of discomfort as she grappled with the idea of becoming the kind of CEO she wanted to be versus other people's perceptions.

You don't know what you don't know, that's OK; everyone else is winging it too

When we interviewed Mandy Bailey, she told us her experience of diving right into an industry that she had no experience of and coming to terms with the notion that she couldn't and wouldn't know everything and was trying to keep up a pretence at the same time.

Mandy Bailey – Plant 'n' Grow

I remember someone saying you don't know what you don't know, and I didn't fully understand what that meant. It's only now, a few years later, that I get that. There is a part of you personally who doesn't want everyone to think you know everything, but you do want people to have confidence that you actually know what you're talking about – but meanwhile you've never done it before. It takes a good while to get comfortable with that – maybe 18 months – to figure out that you don't really know what you're doing.

But then you have to get past that; you can't let it stop you if you get stuck in your head and are always doubting yourself. Sometimes you have to take a step back and trust your own instincts.

Mandy's situation is not unique and 'winging it' is the best-kept secret in the world of entrepreneuring – no one really knows what they're doing. Genuinely. Let's remember the premise of starting a new business is that you're starting something new and it has never been done before. Yes, there might be five companies doing the same thing but not in the same way as you – that's the point. So how can you know for sure what the outcome will be? You can't. And you have to get comfortable with that fact.

We see so many entrepreneurs hold themselves back from the great things that they could be doing because of a fear of getting it wrong, of making mistakes and of failing. There is a great myth that entrepreneurs are great risk-takers but if you meet any successful entrepreneur you will find that the risks are calculated risks: they've weighed up the odds and decided to act on them. Most successful entrepreneurs also have a plan B, C and D and, in reality, spend a huge amount of time mitigating risk. It's rarely 'go big or go home'.

But if you've never done something before, you don't have a lot to go on that is relatable to you. So, you do one of two things. 1) You hold on to your misguided belief that everyone else knows more than you (see point 3 above) and you stop yourself before you do anything too bold or brave or, perish the thought, anything anyone might notice and judge you for. Or 2) You enlist the advice of everyone and their granny, and you end up with so many conflicting viewpoints that you end up in a kind of analysis paralysis.

What if there was a different way? A way to face all of those natural fears and still move forward?

One thing we know to be true is that the entire process of start-up, growth and scale-up is all one big and vulnerable learning curve after the other where you never stop being a beginner. Where every time you think you've mastered something and you're cruising, along comes the next thing that you didn't know that you didn't know yet, and you just have to start the whole process all over again.

And if it's really like this for us and for you, then we can assure you that it really is like this for everyone else too, including everyone we interviewed. Just because no one talks about it doesn't mean that no one else is experiencing it.

In a 2014 article for *The Guardian*, newspaper journalist Oliver Burkeman wrote:

> *We're... shocked whenever authority figures who are supposed to know what they're doing make it plain that they don't. In fact, though, everyone is totally just winging it. We're all... energetically projecting an image of calm proficiency, while inside we're improvising in a mad panic.*[2]

Welcome to the world of *Misadventures in Entrepreneuring*. This is where Tony Robbins was right all along. *This* is where we get to grips with the story that we're telling ourselves in our head and change the way we behave.

This is where we have to turn thoughts like:

---

[2] Oliver Burkeman (21 May 2014), 'Everyone is totally just winging it, all the time', *The Guardian*. Available from: www.theguardian.com/news/ oliver-burkeman-s-blog/2014/may/21/everyone-is-totally-just-winging-it [accessed September 2019].

Burkeman then goes on to cite a popular Reddit thread: 'Grown-ups of Reddit, what is the most embarrassing thing that you should be able to do but can't?' If you ever need to make yourself feel better, then hop on there for a few minutes and after reading about some normal functioning humans that struggle to tie their shoes without 'bunny ears-style', do basic arithmetic at work or pee in public, your day just got a little brighter.

'Everyone else knows what they're doing, and I don't have a clue.'

into

'Everyone is doing their best and maybe we're all just winging it. I should give it a go too.'

And:

'You're such an idiot to think you could compete with people who have been so successful when you have no experience whatsoever.'

into

'Everyone only got successful from being a beginner at some stage, so this is my starting point.'

And:

'You're going to make yourself look stupid.'

into

'Everyone was here once, so what if I don't get it right first time.'

And:

'Let's not bother trying, it seems really difficult (and did we say risky?); let's go back to doing the things we know how to do.'

into

'What would be the downside of just trying?'

When Lucy-Rose and I put out our first podcast, I swear I was nearly sick through fear of public judgement, but we did it anyway. Here's my Instagram post from that day.

> *Today I launched a new podcast with @lucyrosemisadventurers. It was a very exposing and humbling moment and it doesn't matter that I know all the wisdom that says the first anything you do is going to be crap and you just have to be brave and put it out there to get better – it's still scary ass shit and my inner imposter is going crazy! So... to put everything in perspective in between the madness I took my wee dog for a stunning walk at lunch time and remembered just how lucky I am. And regardless of what anyone thinks, I feel brave today. Kind of... *now can someone send me a glass of wine?*

It doesn't matter that I have worked with entrepreneurs for 19 years. It doesn't matter that in the last seven years I directly worked with over 150 entrepreneurs and as a business with over 4,000, I'd never launched a podcast before, and I freaked! It didn't help that I forgot that my Instagram with only 150 followers linked directly to my Facebook where I have over 350 friends who also now know I'm freaking out. And guess what happened? I was flooded with absolutely lovely messages from people encouraging me and celebrating my bold step. And the only way to have known that was to do it.

It's the biggest entrepreneurial conundrum and one of the reasons why we believe that most people don't talk about their real entrepreneuring truth – because they are so afraid that the very people that have faith that they can do this will think less of them if they put themselves out there, show their vulnerability, and say that they don't know what they're doing.

Being able to reframe your beliefs in situations like this and many more can be a really powerful thing. When it comes to vulnerability think about this – have you ever met anyone that you have disrespected, or thought was stupid for being open and honest or vulnerable and asking for help or asking the 'stupid question'? No, me either. Being human and showing that you don't know something (yet) is not a sign of weakness; it's a sign of strength, and a sign of a willingness to learn and grow. What could be more refreshing than that. Yet here we are writing a book about it because not many people in this world do... yet. We'd like to change that, and it starts with reframing our own story.

Course correction questions

- Whose behaviour are you trying to mimic just now in the belief that it will make you successful?
- What are you doing right now, not because you want to, but because you feel you should?
- What are you holding back on because you think that you're not good enough or you're not ready?

What do you need to... Stop, Start and Continue doing now?

STOP

- Believing everything you read and watch about how to be a successful entrepreneur

- Focusing *only* on developing a winning business; instead, work on yourself too

- Second-guessing yourself and trying to be like everyone else – you do you

- Believing that others are better or more experienced than you and worrying that you are the only one winging it

START

- Hanging out with some more relatable role models

- Focusing on developing winning entrepreneurial behaviours

- Figuring out your unique entrepreneurial superpowers and how to do you

---

⊚   Accepting that you don't know everything yet. You're not always going to be perfect, and that's OK

CONTINUE

⊚   Writing your own story, not anyone else's

⊚   Being awesome in ways only you know how

⊚   Trying stuff, experimenting, making mistakes and adventuring!

⊚   Being brave, and vulnerable, even when it scares you

Bonus exercise: Reframing your stories

Reframing is a powerful technique used in Cognitive Behavioural Therapy (CBT) to help when you're telling yourself a story that has the power to hold you back in some way. It enables you to reframe the story to create an alternative outcome.

There are a number of different methods for this. Most of them use a staged process that looks a little like this:

1. Identify the negative or unhelpful story you are telling yourself.
2. Document how the story makes you feel.
3. Sketch multiple alternatives to the story and how you would feel about them.
4. Document any evidence you know to be true to support each alternative.
5. Reflect back on how you now feel about the original story you were telling yourself.

If I had done this about my social media and my fear of public judgement, it might have looked something like this:

1. I am anxious to share that our podcast is now live because I think everyone who listens will think I don't know what I'm talking about, the content is boring, 'who do we think we are launching a podcast?' and lastly, my Scottish accent is really off-putting.
2. This makes me feel exposed, anxious, scared and sick.
3. Alternatives
   - The majority of people who follow us on social media have shown enthusiasm towards our content so far and it will be no different in this instance.
   - Listeners will listen to feel relief and reassurance that they are not alone.
   - Listeners will listen and enjoy the podcast so much that they will share it with their friends and followers.
   - This isn't about me: it's to help others and there is a story to be told.
   - We have existing knowledge and experience that putting something out there and getting feedback is a good way to improve.
4. Evidence
   - The majority of people who follow us on social media are known to us and are supporters. Those that are not known to us have also been positive to date.
   - We have genuine credentials in working with entrepreneurs and each entrepreneur we interviewed said what a relief it was to speak about the content.
   - Those that have heard clips to date have enjoyed listening.
   - No one else is telling this story, or in this way.
5. I now feel that I have no basis for the original story I was telling myself and the unnecessary feelings associated with it. The overwhelming evidence in front of me suggests

that the reaction to our launch will be positive. I also feel that this is an easy technique that I can use to get over a feeling of fear more easily the next time I have one. It won't halt it entirely but will give me a better way to look at the situation objectively and remove some of the emotion and irrationality.

In the end, there really was no grounding in my feelings, and we had 185 listens on the first day. And guess what? No one has ever said anything negative and it turns out hearing Scottish accents is a refreshing change on podcasts.

So, try it out for yourself. There are going to be more of these types of exercises in the pages of this book so why not get yourself a journal or a dedicated notebook to keep them in, or better still, get yourself a *Misadventures in Entrepreneuring Journal.*[3]

---

[3] Specially designed for everyday notes, grand plans, self-awareness exercises, reminders of past screw-ups, reminders of stuff you've been putting off, reminders of things to try, reminders of things never to try again… Available at www.misadventuresinentrepreneuring.com

2

Misadventures in...

USING YOUR COMPASS

In Chapter 1, we discussed not being afraid to be your own version of an entrepreneur, even if it means not knowing everything yet. And we talked about being careful to make sure you were staying true to yourself and not trying to imitate someone else.

So, if you're going to be you – *who are you?*

It's funny how those three little words can have so much power if you really let them unravel.

When was the last time you asked yourself that question? And I don't mean what's your name and where do you come from, or even what's your background, your education or your job history.

I mean underneath all of that superficial stuff, or the historical stuff that shaped you into the person you are today – who actually are you? What do you believe in deep down in your core? What drives you and motivates you? What keeps you awake at night? What do you value in life? What makes you joyful beyond recognition, makes you tick, brings a tear to your eye, makes you angry? Or jealous? Or excited?

If you don't think about this much, then you aren't alone. This level of self-awareness is actually quite rare and if your upbringing and education is in any way similar to ours then it's not something that was given regular focus. Certainly not for the purpose of making bold and profound decisions.

I was talking to a coach the other day, doing a little self-assessment of the last decade. We both agreed that in our worlds the last decade seems to have been the decade of personal growth. Suddenly over the last 10 years everyone has been talking about self-development, personality profiling, mindset and coaching – things that used to just be the realms of sport and life are now an integral part of business today.

And if you feel a little at sea with it all I don't blame you.

About five years ago, I was having a conversation with a friend and I was discussing running a team. I was struggling a little bit with some of the team members and how to communicate my expectations to them. My friend very eloquently waved her wine glass at me and said: 'But how can you expect them to know what you're expecting when they don't know who (the f*ck) you are...?'

I was a bit taken aback: 'What do you mean?' I asked.

'Well, who are you? What do you believe in? What are your values? And what are your standards and expectations of them?' she replied.

Still taken aback, I listened for a while as she explained from her PR background the importance of having a position in life. Not a role or a title, but a standpoint that I believed deep in my core, and that I lived by. Like a personal manifesto. She explained further that most people have this, but they don't really know what it is or how to articulate it. And without being clear on it, they find it difficult to communicate to everyone else. This can lead to finding yourself making decisions or saying yes (or no) to things that don't necessarily *feel* right.

I let this sink in for a minute. Of course, it made perfect sense that if I wasn't clear on who I was and all of those things she described, then how could I expect anyone else to be?

I set off on a mission – Project Who-the-f*ck-is-Gayle. All of a sudden, I was questioning my opinions – did I even have them? This was a minefield. I asked my partner and he said I had to stand up for my beliefs more and that having opinions was a good thing.

'Where do I get them from?' I asked.

'Try listening to Radio 4?' he replied.

It turns out this was actually a good move and very quickly I revealed my first strong opinion... that I was definitely *not* a Radio 4 listener.

It became almost like an obsession, to reveal the real me, and it was exhausting. I was going around in circles testing out new opinions through trial and error and having all sorts of misadventures. What I really needed was a starting point – something that made sense that I could hold on to that really felt like me. My true north.

What I needed was a compass – a device for finding direction with a needle that *always* pointed to my true north even when everything around me was moving or unknown.

Let's talk about the compass for a second. The compass was a dramatic advancement in navigation that allowed sailors to find their way even if clouds obscured the stars, which were their normal navigational tool. Before the compass there was no way of knowing where you were in open seas, or which way you were pointing. The compass at last enabled worldwide travel without the limits of following the land or the weather. You could say that the compass, followed by an explorer's desire to follow it, changed the course of human history. Does this sound familiar?

This is what I needed; we all do. Entrepreneuring is no less unchartered waters than those of early mariners, unknown and prone to change – and we all need some way to navigate this in a way that works for us. Following someone else's way markers only gets you so far.

Have you tuned in to your own internal compass lately? It is such a great way to help us find what feels like true north when it seems like we might have got lost somewhere along the way.

My quest began with figuring out how this shaped my values and the things I believed in – the kind of stuff I wasn't willing to compromise on. That helped me to create a vision for myself and it has helped me to make life decisions. Values are fundamental, and I was kicking myself for not discovering this sooner – but you don't know what you don't know, right?

In this chapter, we're going to help you to dig a bit deeper past all the superficial stuff you already know and into the stuff that you haven't thought about for a while, or maybe ever. We're starting with identifying our values and taking them from a theoretical bit of paper that you once did on a training course, and we're looking at how they can really supercharge your decision making (ignore them at your peril). Then we'll look at how we can use these as a starting point to really set you off in the right direction with a clear vision for *your own* road less travelled, not following someone else's path.

Perhaps we're going to reveal some magically or scarily unknown insights, or at the very least give some added confidence that you're being entirely yourself, as daunting as that may feel.

Values that guide you

Values, it seems, are quite badass. They have the power to make you feel excellent if you stick with them, and a bit crappy when you don't. You know that feeling of something just not 'feeling right' or niggling or gnawing at you and you can't quite put your finger on why it doesn't sit well? There's a good chance it's because you've compromised a value somewhere. Maybe just a little, but a compromise none the less, and a voice inside your head (and your gut) is trying to tell you something. A bit like when you decide to ignore the sat nav and take a different route and it insists on a U-turn for an indeterminate amount of time.

Values are a set of parameters there to guide your behaviour and your decisions. Get them right and you'll be swift and focused in your decision making with clear direction. Get them wrong or leave them ambiguous, and you'll constantly wonder how you got into situations where something just doesn't sit right with you.

Consciously or unconsciously, we use our personal values to pick friends, relationships and careers. Your values also help you manage things like time and money – they help you to decide to spend these on things that are ultimately going to make you the happiest.

What's all this got to do with misadventures in entrepreneuring? Actually, a lot. Think back to the last time you made a decision in business and it didn't feel quite right. Ever uttered the words 'I wish I'd gone with my gut on that'? I'll bet you can trace it back to a value.

Using your values to guide your decisions as an entrepreneur will help you to avoid all kinds of misadventures. Choose to ignore them and you might find yourself in a place that you never expected.

Let me give you some examples of when following values can really make a difference.

Values in choosing a co-founder

When we interviewed Gary Butterfield of Everyday Juice Limited, he told us how starting with values impacted him and his business partner and how they used values to guide more than their relationship.

> *There's never been an occasion when Andy and I have clashed because we sat in a bar in north Leeds and wrote down on the back of a napkin what we wanted the values to be. It's the old beer mat business plan; we both developed the concept together, those values, and what we wanted the concept to look like. Because we did that together we always know what we're working towards and we're always, always on the same page.*

> *Everything we do is values driven. Even when it comes to our products we totally buy into the 'starting with why' concept and so we look at the problem that we are going to solve and why we're doing that, and the money comes later.*

Whenever more than one person is involved in a decision-making process, there is always potential for a difference in opinion to occur that could lead to a head-to-head or a stalemate situation. Using your values to guide your decisions can really help ensure you and your co-founder are on the same page and that values come first.

Values in working with suppliers and customers

Values also work for your business. You can take your personal values and extend them to your brand and your company so that everyone you interact with understands who you are and what you believe in.

Mandy Bailey from Plant 'n' Grow told us about a time she really had to put her values to work and make some hard, commercial decisions to protect her brand because her gut wouldn't let her do otherwise.

> *You have to pick and choose your customers wisely. We've said no to a few big customers, which I know would have brought us great volume and even some very short-term profit, but would have caused us a lot of pain further down. One in particular was a £30k order earlier this year. It would just have been amazing for us – and we just had to say no because it would have compromised our brand moving forward.*
>
> *You have to go back to your values all the time and if your gut is telling you that straight away 'oh my goodness that would be so amazing but there's just something that's not right about that', then you have to pick away at what it is that doesn't feel right. And you have to think, as good as the cash would be and it would help us right at this moment*

and put us on a great footing, it's not the right thing for our brand and would hurt us further down the line and compromise the next stage of our growth.

So, it all comes back to values and where is the right place and who is our customer? Because that's the thing I have found bizarre – we're pretty clear now on who our customer is, and who our second and third customers are, but I find it amazing that engaging with some retailers and we're clear about our customer, and saying – we don't think this is right for you – they still want our product?

It's not an easy road when you can see an opportunity and you can see the lost sales. I remember telling a mentor that I had turned down the order and it really hurt but I knew it was the right thing. She said, 'that's your values in action, that's what they're there to do'. It really hurt but I knew it would hurt more to regret it, and it's something I'm really proud of doing.

If it means we grow a bit slower, then that's what we'll do.

When you are starting out, it is really hard to imagine that customers could be bad for business or that there would be any benefit from saying no to someone. When Lauren Valler of Habakuk Recruitment took on a customer that didn't share the same values, she quickly found out to her detriment the impact that could have.

I just realized in business as much as we try to be ethical, there are people out there who are not ethical. I should have done better diligence. We worked with one company who let our candidates down quite often. I probably should have said no at that point but you're just so far into it and as a start-up business you feel like you have to accept the business, as it's revenue in!

I should have stuck to my values. They owed us £7,000 and we were chasing them. We then found out they were going into liquidation. It's learning from those mistakes: any company we now work with I now investigate, I was naive early on. I work now with corporates as it's stereotyped smaller businesses for me, which I know is wrong. Now I use that gut feel; I knew something was not right and I didn't listen to it. I check they have a fair reputation and good practice.

Values in culture

Ever since marketing companies started putting ping pong tables in staffrooms and Facebook and Google started offering free fruit or slides to get from one floor of the office to the other, the idea of building a great culture in the workplace has grown arms and legs. Bookshop shelves are groaning with titles on it, change consultants are quids in on the topic, and hungry start-up CEOs are clamouring to attract and retain talent by showcasing a top-notch culture.

And if you are making your first couple of hires, then creating and maintaining a culture that excites and engages people can be a bit of a daunting process. Made even more challenging by the fact that most of that bike riding and free fruit stuff is bullsh*t.

Culture isn't a material thing; you can't buy it or give it or paint the walls in it. The good news is that when you boil it down, culture is actually a pretty straightforward concept, particularly if you've done your work on your values.

Culture is about having a strong understanding of your beliefs and values and then living them every day in your life and work. You build a culture with your team by communicating those beliefs and values and asking them to commit to living by them as well.

We used to have a phrase in Entrepreneurial Spark that we used to ask ourselves about whether or not we believed someone was living the values of the business. We would ask ourselves: 'Are they in the canoe with us and paddling in the same direction, or are they drilling holes?' It was a powerful question and we would know right away if someone had departed from our values and was drilling holes in our culture.

If you're not sure about how to implement your values in your business to build your culture, then it can be helpful to get specific about what it means to live them as this will determine your expectations when it comes to how you and everyone else behaves towards one another and towards your customers.

Daniel Marcos – Growth Institute

I make sure I have a daily huddle across all of our remote locations for 7–12 minutes per day. This is my only cooler time with everyone on video; we look like the Brady bunch with all 30 of us on the webcams.

I only visit the offices once a month and I believe the CEO should not have an office in the office: our role is to make things happen. We are in co-working spaces and I need to get a permit when I visit our office. I work in a conference room all day and my employees come in and see me – I am there to serve them. Then when I am at my home office, I do my execution. My role is not the operation; I am out there selling. When I work with CEOs they think they should be in the office 24/7 but they need to be out there building the business.

Values in your hiring process

There are loads of ways to set expectations and test for a value fit in your hiring process. I hadn't even considered these until we started to grow Entrepreneurial Spark. About two years into our journey, we reviewed our entire recruitment process because we were about to enter a period of rapid growth, hiring up to eight team members for three new locations every six months for three years.

Up until this point we'd never put our finger on what made our team so special. So we set about defining what it was about us and the way we worked that we loved, as well as what we believed we wanted from our new team. We rewrote job descriptions to include phrases like 'here's the nitty gritty' and 'please give us 200 words on why you're a rockstar'. Honesty and transparency were in our value set – actually the phrase we used was 'no elephants left in the room' but you get the picture.

We brought in an assessment day that we called Bootcamp and we asked candidates to tell us about entrepreneurs who inspired them. We sent them pre-assessment information that included headshots of the recruitment team with details of the type of people we were and what made us happy (mostly cheese and doughnut related). Our aim was to enable our candidates to get to know us as much as we were about to get to know them.

I'm pleased to say it worked for us. By creating a process that was explicit about our values and specifically designed to showcase the values of our candidates, we were able to get a much better idea of who we were actually going to hire, rather than some polished interview performance. We wanted to give them a good experience, and we wanted to find someone who wanted us as much as we wanted them.

It also made our recruitment Bootcamps fun for everyone involved. We felt that if someone was going to take a day out of their lives to come and try out to be part of our team, then that was the least that we could give them in return. In fact, on one occasion all 12 candidates went to the pub together at the end of the day!

Mel Bound – This Mum Runs

Hiring has been the hardest thing and the most important thing for my business, but also one you can easily get wrong. In the very early stages when you don't have all the structures and strategy in place, you just have a shed-load of work and you just need folk to help you with it but you can't pay them very much; you don't really feel like you have the luxury of time to plan a recruitment process.

When I crowdfunded, I was a bit clearer on where the business was going, and we were at that point we had a bit of money and I really wanted to put more structure around recruitment. The first thing we did was to look at how we could recruit on values rather than experience.

We put people through a really rigorous process, and it took us months; there were several stages, one-to-one interviews, short listing, etc. However, when you're up against it, it can be really tempting to ignore your own process and try to fill a short-term need rather than maintaining a long-term view, hiring slow and sticking to your values. And even with the best processes in the world, my gut and my internal compass have never been wrong (even if I haven't always listened to them!).

Don't be afraid to tear up the hiring process rulebook. It's *your* process and if you want to know about their values – just ask! If any of your values are compromised during the process, then you'll know it's not meant to be. Don't be inclined to do it anyway.

Values in your internal communications

The trick to ensuring values are lived every day in your culture is to bring them to life in as many ways as you can. At Entrepreneurial Spark we had ours designed, printed and framed and we gave them to every member of staff. Whenever they were unsure about a course of action, this gave them a guidance point that meant they never had to second guess the response of their colleagues, their line managers or the directors of the business.

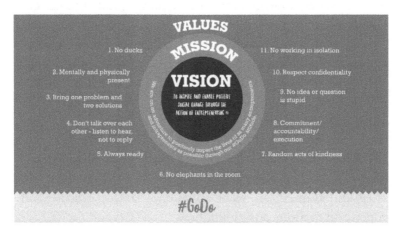

Our team worked across 13 different locations so making sure that they were as connected to the business and their teammates as they could be was crucial to us – no working in isolation. We introduced a weekly internal communications email that went out to everyone in the business once a week called 'In The Loop' – we used this to communicate important team-wide information as well as fun informal stuff.

We also used the values in performance reviews. As you can probably guess, we didn't do performance reviews like most people and checked in with our staff as regularly as we could, both formally and informally. When we were at our largest, we had 44 members of staff and Lucy-Rose made a point of checking in with every single one of them regularly. It was amazing to see the power of a text from the CEO to ask how your bike ride at the weekend went, or if you had enjoyed your holiday. When you actually care, and you behave like you care, then your team are motivated to care too.

The power of knowing and living by those values really shines when you consider that we had a team of over 40 and no dedicated HR function, ever. We just tended to make it up as we went along and got it right more times than not. When the team suggested a flexible working plan, we decided to get out a blank piece of paper at our away days and all do it together. We asked them what was important to them and how could we achieve this while still supporting our customers and partners. They then had ownership of the new plan moving forward. We used our gut to feel our way through, treating our team as adults and not numbers. We cared.

This kind of care and attention also made it easier to ask our team to be mentally and physically present, to always be ready, to ask stupid questions, to be accountable and to execute, and to perform random acts of kindness.

Top tips for getting clarity on your values

1. *Do a values exercise* (hint: there's one at the end of this chapter) – Many people claim to understand their own values; however, if you haven't done a values exercise before or need a refresher it's worth doing one to help reinforce your thinking and articulate your values in writing. This

will help to ensure you are absolutely clear before testing them through daily decision making.

2. *Do as many as you need until you're clear* – If our exercise doesn't get you to the result you need, then you only have to hop on the internet to find different methods. In the end, you should have a list of values that should be reflective of the times where you acted in a way that you were truly happy, proud or fulfilled in life, and in a way that your gut didn't grumble about.

3. *Rank them* – It can also be helpful to create a hierarchy or rank your values in case you ever find yourself in situations where you might have to compromise one over the other.

4. *Test them* – It is often not until our values are truly tested and we are asked to compromise one that we recognize our true self. A simple way to do this is to take each value in turn and ask yourself the following questions:

- Have I ever compromised this value?
- How did it make me feel?
- Knowing what I know now, would I be prepared to compromise that value again?
- Under what circumstances did I/would I be prepared to compromise?
- Would I be prepared to end a friendship if someone in my life asked me to compromise my values?
- Would I be prepared to resign from my job if my employer asked me to compromise my values?

By putting these to the test, this should help you to determine how strongly you feel about each one, and also what you may have learned having compromised any in the past. Did it make you feel more strongly about it, or did it make you realize there are more important things in life?

Once you are clearer on your values, you've got a rock-solid guidance tool to come back to if you ever feel lost. We'll refer back to values quite a lot in the remainder of the book. As we said before, going against these can be the root cause of many misadventures.

If you don't know where you're going, how do you know when you get there?

Now you've got a framework for making decisions that you can feel comfortable with, this can help you navigate your way towards a clearer vision. That is, you can begin to envision your destination for your business – not the road map of course – you're going to make that one up as you go along.

Your vision, however, is something to work towards – to point your compass at. I know this might seem fairly obvious to some, but I had never created any kind of vision before I came to Entrepreneurial Spark. I bet most of you haven't either unless you've had some kind of coaching. And they're not just for business; they're for life too.

As a coach, Lucy-Rose loves nothing more than to sit down with a vision board at the start of each new year and project herself into the future. She likes to think about how life is going to feel, focus on what her surroundings will look like and what everyday life will be like. Then she creates a visual representation of what it's going to look like. For her, it's about understanding her values and purpose and where she would like them to take her.

I'm not one to believe in manifestation but in 2010 Lucy-Rose created a vision board before she had even heard of Entrepreneurial Spark. When she unearthed it in 2014, she had actually drawn a scarily accurate picture of the building we located the first accelerator hub in, even using the word 'Hub', the name we called our HQ team, on the board.

Lucy-Rose's top tips for creating a vision of your own

If you have never taken the time to create a vision of your own, then here are Lucy-Rose's top tips. If you're a visual person you can also turn this into a vision board like she did.

1. Write the word 'Draft' at the top – no need to fix this right away.
2. Pick the time frame and picture the scene.
3. Send yourself to the future – what will your world look and feel like a year from now?
4. Go for something big! It might feel unachievable right now but that's the point.
5. Write from the heart. It can also be words and pictures you draw and cut or print out.
6. Write quickly – hot pen! Don't self-edit.
7. Don't be afraid to get personal about all areas of your life.
8. Be very specific – how will you feel? What will you see?
9. Remember to capture your values.
10. Review and re-draft on a big sheet or board that you can see regularly.
11. Get input from others – how do they fit in and how can they support you?
12. Get going! Time to take action. What is the first baby step?

There are loads of different ways to create a vision for yourself and your business and some people are more comfortable doing it than others. I am a very visual person but despite having a vision in my mind for *Misadventures in Entrepreneuring*, I can't seem to get it down on paper – but for you I'm going to try.

When I began writing this book and to this day, I can close my eyes and I have a crystal-clear picture in my mind...

It is you, with a copy of this book. It's well-thumbed and you found it when an entrepreneur friend thought it was exactly what you needed. Or you passed through the business section of the bookshop or, better still, the 'fresh thinking' section and it caught your eye. In fact, it stood out because you've never seen a 'business' book that looks more like an adventure book before. You are intrigued because it makes a refreshing change from all of the stark book jackets in primary colours shouting at you with their angry bold fonts, or their rocket images.

The word 'misadventure' intrigues you and you read the back cover and you discover that all this abnormality actually comes with a fair bit of credibility. Perhaps these women and the 4,000 entrepreneurs they've worked with know what they're talking about? And you're thinking: 'Isn't it lovely that they speak a language I can understand.'

By the time you've finished the book, you've laughed, you've cried, you've been shocked by some of the stories and comforted by others. Your overwhelming feeling is one of thank goodness I'm not alone, thank goodness this is normal, and thank goodness someone decided to write about it.

Now your book sits on the desk, or the bookshelf not too far away as a reminder that you're going to have misadventures, lots of them, and you'll be OK. I also like to think that we've inspired you into some moments of bravery, and to know yourself better than you ever have, so you can create that life you really want.

Maybe you'll pass the book on? Or recommend it to someone else that you know probably feels a lot like you. In my vision you feel that, because you have taken something from it, you want to pay it forward to someone else.

That is my vision for this book and where I'm going with it, and it's with that destination in mind that I sit down to write every day. Without it I would be lost, and my writing would be meaningless.

I hold on to that destination point and it stops me veering wildly off course on days when the road map to getting there doesn't look like I envisaged it! When things change, when I don't feel like writing or the task seems impossible. Or on the days when I wake up crippled by the prospect of judgement and the fear that I'll help no one.

It all comes back to being able to draw on my values and my vision to determine how to approach every day, how I write the book and how I want you to feel when you see it, buy it, receive it, read it or pass it on. Those things combined allow me to create a clear and purposeful way forward rather than getting stuck, or worse, letting the fear stop me from getting there.

Course correction questions

- Who are you really? How do you know?
- Where in your life or business are you compromising on your values and what has to change?
- When did you last go against a gut feeling and what did you learn?

What do you need to... Stop, Start and Continue doing now?

STOP

- Trying to be someone you're not

- Compromising on your values

- Making decisions based on flawed criteria

- Going against your gut

START

- Getting to know the real you

- Getting clear values and finding your true north

- Setting a vision for yourself

- Following your internal compass

- Trusting your compass to lead you to the right outcomes

CONTINUE

- Trusting your gut

- Getting to know yourself

- Being authentically you

Bonus exercise 1: Get started with your values

Simply sitting down with a blank sheet of paper and writing your values down is hard! Sometimes it's a gut feeling that you haven't been able to put into words, or a situation that just felt right (or wrong). But putting a label on that feeling isn't a straightforward thing.

Most values exercises start with a big long list of words that describe values, which can be helpful to an extent. But I bet if I were to ask you to look at the following list you could probably look at all of the words and say, yes, you value them to a certain degree.

When I was doing this for myself, I needed a clearer place to start. I found that beginning with the people in my life who I admire or who inspire me and ultimately shaped my belief systems was a really useful first step. I wrote a list of the ones that really stuck out and why. Here's a sample of mine:

Family	Mum	Selflessness
		Bravery with humility
		Adventurousness
		Hard-working
		Integrity
		Honesty
	Dad	Fearlessness
		Indefatigability/challenge the status quo
		Hard-working
		Ingenuity
		Confidence

	Aunt	Kindness
		Thoughtfulness
		Bravery with humility
		High standards (for themselves and others)
		Honesty
Friends/ colleagues	I'll spare their blushes – but it's a big list made up of incredible people	Positivity
		Confidence
		Hard-working
		Serious, not serious
		High standards (for themselves and others)
		Courage of conviction
		Integrity
		Compassion
		Badass
		Creativity/ingenuity
		Challenge the status quo
		Fearlessness
		Honesty
Celebrities Sportspeople Entrepreneurs Others		Hard work/dedication
		Striving to be the best
		Unafraid/proud of being different
		Ingenuity
		Bravery with humility
		Compassion and kindness

You can see from the list that there are a good few overlapping words and themes that came through strongly. Hard work is one that shines bright every time I do this, and I am proud that this is a pillar of my value system. At the same time, I recognize that I can also place an unrealistic amount of importance on the effort that I expect from anyone I work with. This can cause problems when I am working with others and I don't believe they are living up to the bar I have set in my head. This can also cause me to put undue pressure on myself and others to achieve more than is sensible.

The positive news is that I do recognize this and have worked hard over the years to understand where this value comes from and how I can use it as a force for good and not as a slave driver!

Once you have a long list, you can then take a list like the one that follows and compare and contrast with what you already have. The aim is to select up to 10 that you think stand out more than others. You might also find by doing this you realize there is something missing from the list that you feel strongly about. Add it to your 10.[4]

When you have your list, you should be able to look at it and agree that the values are reflective of the times when you acted in such a way that you were truly happy, proud or fulfilled in life.

Abundance	Accountability	Achievement	Action
Adventure	Ambition	Awareness	Balance
Beauty	Being the Best	Calmness	Cheerfulness
Clarity	Comfort	Compassion	Competition
Connection	Contribution	Control	Courage
Creativity	Curiosity	Determination	Discipline

---

[4] Ten is an arbitrary number. It really doesn't matter how many you have at this stage; it's a narrowing-down process from an infinite number of options. Feel free to pick your own number.

Effectiveness	Empathy	Energy	Enthusiasm
Excellence	Fairness	Faith	Fame
Family	Flexibility	Freedom	Friendship
Fulfilment	Fun	Happiness	Harmony
Health	Honesty	Honour	Humility
Independence	Inspiration	Integrity	Intelligence
Intimacy	Kindness	Knowledge	Liveliness
Love	Money	Nature	Passion
Peace	Perfection	Persistence	Philanthropy
Power	Respect	Security	Significance
Simplicity	Spirituality	Spontaneity	Stability
Status	Strength	Success	Teamwork
Tolerance	Tradition	Truth	Vitality
Wealth	Wisdom		

Write your top 10 here:

1. _____

2. _____

3. _____

4. _____

5. _____

6. _____

7. _____

8. _____

9. _____

10. _____

Bonus exercise 2: Create your values hierarchy

One reason for creating a hierarchy or ranking our values is that we can often find ourselves in situations when we have to compromise on our values. These can be difficult decisions driven by powerful emotions. By looking at the values you feel are more important than others when you're in an unemotional state, you can filter out some of the less important ones. Do this by starting at the top and comparing each one in turn with all of the others, asking yourself: 'If I had to choose between them which one would I choose?' Do this for all 10 until you have an ordered list.

e.g. If I had to compare Hard Work and Honesty, then I would definitely rank Honesty above Hard Work, but if I had to compare Hard Work and Selflessness, I would rank Hard Work higher than Selflessness.

Write your values hierarchy here:

1. _____

2. _____

3. _____

4. _____

5. _____

6. _____

7. _____

8. _____

9. _____

10. _____

Bonus exercise 3: Testing your values and applying them in the real world

Before you go out into the world and apply your values to everything you see, it can be a good idea to test them! Sometimes what you think you believe strongly in will buckle under the weight of a real-life situation. It's time to think back to some situations where these values might have been tested in the past and be really honest with yourself.

This is particularly important to help you distinguish between the person you are and the person you wish you were. Often, we choose values that we aspire to but, in reality, we would behave differently. How do your values shore up when you apply a little pressure?

Ask yourself the questions we looked at earlier in the chapter:

- ⓐ Have I ever compromised this value?
- ⓐ How did it make me feel?
- ⓐ Knowing what I know now, would I be prepared to compromise that value again?
- ⓐ Under what circumstances did you/would you be prepared to compromise?
- ⓐ Would I be prepared to end a friendship if someone in my life asked me to compromise my values?
- ⓐ Would I be prepared to resign from my job if my employer asked me to compromise my values?
- ⓐ Is there one value in particular I would do this for?

By the end of these three exercises, you should have a really good idea of the ideals that are important to you in life and that guide your decisions. Nevertheless, as we evolve over time this list will also evolve. It's important to revisit this list from time to time and see if they still ring true to you. This is particularly important if this is the first time you have done this. Let them sit for a while until you are comfortable that this is what you stand for. Once you have done this, you will find a new level of confidence to go out there and let the world know what to expect from you.

3

Misadventures in...

PASSION

Getting to know yourself better and understanding how to find your true north is going to give you a great base to build on. Now you can start to understand the kind of attributes that would be helpful to develop and begin to really unlock your superpowers. If, like us, you've spent a lot of time learning about what attributes make a great entrepreneur, you are bound to have come across the word 'passion' more often than not. Most probably in phrases like:

> *'Successful entrepreneurs find something that they are passionate about and put their heart and soul into doing it.'*

> *'It was their passion about x that really bowled us over.'*

> *'They were so passionate about x that they wouldn't stop until they made something happen.'*

We've heard it said so often that we could have been fooled into believing that passion itself could be *the* most important characteristic of a successful entrepreneur, but we weren't wholly convinced.

Now, not even we can argue that in an ideal universe we'd all be doing the things we love or are most passionate about all day every day. Even the notion of 'work' has had a bit of an image overhaul in the last 20 or so years and unlike our grandparents' generation, or even our parents' generation, you no longer have to choose a profession because it's noble or your civic duty or will enable you to provide for your family.

But what is it about passion? Can it make that crucial difference between success and failure? Or is it something to be used wisely? In this chapter, we're going to look at when we believe passion can set you apart from the competition, when it can cause you to misadventure, how it can affect your mindset and even your mental health, and if you can have too much of a good thing.

A cautionary tale of passion

The first thing we should say about passion is that we believe the word itself is highly overused and generally misunderstood. For the last decade, the word passion has become the way for job-seekers and entrepreneurs to describe how they feel about pretty much everything. And to identify themselves as more eager or enthusiastic than the next person in order to secure that job or that investment.

The word is also so frequently used that it has started to lose its meaning. In recent years, LinkedIn has published a list of the most overused buzzwords that appear in their user profiles, and without fail 'passionate' is up there every time. In fact, it moved from fourth to third position in 2017,[5] and every year

---

[5] You should also check out the other words on the buzzword list to see what crimes you may be committing in your user profile. It's surprisingly hard to banish them all and you have to get pretty creative to be original!

Blair Heitmann (25 January 2017), 'You're better than buzzwords – Start showing it', *LinkedIn*. Available from: https://blog.linkedin.com/2017/january/25/better-than-buzzwords-2017-is-the-year-to-start-showing-it-linkedin [accessed June 2018].

the site actively discourages users from its inclusion for fear of them seeming ordinary or even common – ironically, the very opposite of differentiating themselves.

For me, it has lost so much meaning that it now goes on the list of adjectives that would actually put me off someone, rather than finding them attractive to work with. In the same way as 'cool' or 'awesome' give me an involuntary twitch. And what worries me even more than the nails on the blackboard effect of the word is that its overuse actually detracts from the true nature of what it means to be passionate.

Like one of my other most irksome words, 'awesome' – defined as something that inspires awe – the impact of these words has been diluted in our culture by their adoption into our everyday vocabulary, and they become meaningless. When was the last time that you can honestly say that something inspired true awe in you?

To get to grips with why passion is so important, we need to look at when it really matters.

When passion gets you out of bed in the morning

We've all been there: the Sunday dread of the Monday morning. The smugness of the Insta-generation and their endless stream of messages that tell us to find work that we don't need to vacation from. Of course, that's what we're all looking for. No one wants their work to feel like a grind. Yet a lot of us continue to do what we have to over what we'd like to, because we don't yet know that there is another way.

And we have to admire those that choose to swim against the Monday morning nine to five tide and find or create work that doesn't feel like work. Wouldn't that be exciting, to actually want to leap out of bed in the morning? For work not to feel like work. To genuinely be doing something that you love to do every day, or that makes you feel like you are serving a higher purpose? It's a far greater motivator than having a job for a job's sake.

I don't know about you but I'm only on this planet once; I want to make it my business to make sure I'm loving every minute of it. Having worked with over 4,000 entrepreneurs, they also agree. Some of the most common reasons to become an entrepreneur that we saw were:

- To solve a problem (yours or someone else's).
- To do something fulfilling (gets you out of bed in the morning).
- To follow your purpose (do what you were put on the planet to do).
- To right an injustice.
- To create positive change in the world.

The funny thing is I don't believe a lot of people know they need real passion in their lives until they actually experience it. I worked in jobs in the past that I enjoyed, and I worked hard. It wasn't until I went to Entrepreneurial Spark that I recognized that this was something different. It now feels unthinkable to be doing anything that doesn't give me that same feeling every day.

Paul Adams – Goldfish London

> I started a side business in credit control. I had a team and they made all the calls; we had to take people to the small claims if they weren't paying, that kind of thing. It was a nicely ticking over little thing, but it taught me that you don't ever start a business that's boring. Chasing people

*for money and it's not even my money; it was so boring. I
would call in sick on a Monday and I was the boss and I
couldn't face it. Never start a business that if it succeeds:
you'd be unhappy doing it. It might pay the bills, but you've
got to actually enjoy it.*

This is the kind of passion that is going to make a difference
to your business – the kind that gets you out of bed in the
morning more than anything else does because you simply can't
bear to waste a minute doing anything else.

When passion gets you through the tough times

It stands to reason that if you are doing something you love
every day and it doesn't really feel like work, then naturally you
are going to have more time, energy and enthusiasm to give to
it. We've met so many entrepreneurs that say that having their
own business is 'sooooo hard' *but* 'it's a different kind of hard'.
They say that it's a kind of hard that you wouldn't put up with
working for anyone else, but if it's for yourself, it's an adrenaline
rush and it means something different, especially if it's for the
greater good too.

Lynn White – Talent on Leave

*I've been managing my anxiety as I go along with daily
rituals and reminders. With the help of grandparents, I
take care of the children with my husband working full
time. The exhausting part can be the constant buffering.
I have often reassessed why I'm doing this and who I'm
doing it for. There are easier ways to make a living, but
I have found an inner strength from I don't know where
except that this feels like my space in life, what I'm meant
to be doing. If I didn't have the passion I have, I would*

have given up 100 times before as it's just so hard with the volume and the juggling.

Likewise, when things get tough, there's nothing like being passionate to get you through the hard times in a way that money never would. We've met countless entrepreneurs that have turned their back on big salaries because they were so unfulfilled by what they were doing that no money in the world would make them happy doing it.

Now before you scoff, I agree that's really easy to say when you've got money and are in a privileged position to be able to do that. But we've also met countless entrepreneurs who are so driven by their passion that they'll get out of bed to go and do what they love, even if it makes them no money. In fact, entrepreneur Roger Hamilton, author of *The Millionaire Masterplan*,[6] believes that passions are actually things we tend to *spend* money on, rather than make money out of.

Emma Baylin of Shared Harmonies, has combined all her passions to create her business and although it has been really tough, she knew it was the only thing she wanted to do:

> *I had a real passion for things that improve health and wellbeing; I had a real passion for working with people who don't access mainstream health services. I'm a youth and community worker, and therefore have a passion for things that form that sense of community. I also have had a lifetime passion for singing. I wanted to bring them all together and create a business.*
>
> *I didn't know what the business would look like in the beginning, but I knew I wanted to work out in communities.*

---

[6] Roger Hamilton (2014), *The Millionaire Masterplan*, Business Plus.

I started working with people who struggle with mental health problems. I realized I needed a way to make that business sustainable; the majority of people who accessed my services couldn't pay for it and I didn't want to charge those people and I wanted to keep it on a donation basis. Businesses were just starting to recognize the importance of wellbeing in the workplace and I realized corporate business would also benefit, and that kind of work could subsidize the community work.

I stayed in employment for the first four years whilst I started the business and never really got the chance to develop the corporate work as I focused on the community side, which meant the business was costing me money! No matter how difficult running the business was, it had always been a pleasure in contrast to the full-time role I'd had to go back to, where there was an element of increasing uncomfortableness and which had become more and more stressful. I had to make a decision – either that the business was a pleasurable pastime and reduce my time on it, or I needed to wholeheartedly put everything into it and make it work. So, at the point of turning 40 I decided to take the plunge.

The kind of passion that is going to make a difference to your business is the kind of passion that gets you through the tough times instead of giving up.

When passion helps you to go places others don't understand

When you're truly passionate about the concept of your business, then you know it inside and out and you understand the customer pain point better than anyone. Perhaps you were that customer, you have experienced that pain, or you've seen someone you love experience it. As we've mentioned before, perhaps it's an injustice that you've observed that really hit you right in your value set and you've made it your business to find out more or make it better.

Or, perhaps you're just one of these magical creatures that wakes up every morning with a deep-seated dissatisfaction with the way that the world works (or even just a tiny microcosm of it) and an unstoppable desire to fix it. Whatever it is, you are going to go places that the passives, the apathetic, the indifferent or the downright lazy are not going to go. You will create a better product or service than the next person because you understand the customer and what they need, and you feel their pain and want to fix it in a more fulfilling way than you've seen it be done to date.

This not only means you will create better products and services, but it also means you have the heart to motivate others towards a common goal. Passion radiates out of you to the point that others have no option but to rally around your cause. You can motivate them to be as passionate as you, and you can lead a team to success.

The kind of passion that is going to make a difference to your business is the kind of passion that drives you to stay curious, creative, innovative and seek new solutions to problems over and over again. To go beyond your comfort zone to understand the real root of customer problems and address them. And not see less or be blinded by your assumptions.

Matt Kandela of Dear Future, has recognized the need to stay curious as a business owner.

When you're working for a big company, you're always trying to validate their business model. They have a way of doing things and you need to convince clients that is the right way. But when you run your own business, and if you're going to be successful, you always have to seek to disprove your business model and always try to find new ways to do things. Should we move into this space, should we do this rather than that, should we improve our hiring process. We are a small team so we can make those decisions often and quickly.

Passion is a heady cocktail of emotion as well as drive and determination that allows you to push forward, break boundaries and find your way around the barriers and obstacles put in your way. It is this infectiousness that causes people to get excited.

Misadventures of passion

But... and this is a big *but...* passion alone doesn't make you a great entrepreneur, or mean you'll have a successful business. And while there are a huge number of benefits to being passionate, it does have its occasional downsides.

It's driven by emotion.

If you've ever looked up the definition of passion in the dictionary,[7] you'll find a few more definitions that are troubling when applying them to growing a business.

1. mass noun Strong and barely controllable emotion.

I'm going to say that if we went back to successful entrepreneurs, professors and investors and asked them if it was strong and

---

[7] Oxford University Press (2019), 'What does passion mean?', *Lexico*. Available from: www.lexico.com/en/definition/passion [accessed August 2019].

barely controllable emotions that were the root of all success in business, they may have a different opinion.

2. in singular A state or outburst of strong emotion.

Emotions are great in business: they keep you grounded, they stop you from seeing everything in black and white, they help you to empathize with customers and staff alike. But I would be worried if you relied upon strong emotions to make sound business decisions.

Ben Treleaven – ISO Spaces

This business looks to me like a spreadsheet with numbers; I have zero emotional attachment to it, and I think that works really well. I meet a lot of entrepreneurs who are so hung up on their business, they truly believe in their product above anything else. Don't get me wrong, I really like our product and I know it is serving a need. But if you become emotionally attached to your product or service you can end up flogging a dead horse if it's not working. Whereas we can say we've done that, and it didn't work, so let's try it this way instead.

The kind of passion that is going to make a difference to your business is the kind of passion that recognizes when to engage your heart, and when to engage your head for the greater good of your business and your customer.

It's blinding

When it's personal, we can become blinded to all sorts of truths or facts that we choose not to see because we believe so intensely in what we're doing.

This can lead us to all sorts of misadventures. Like:

- Believing that because you are so passionate about the problem *you* have experienced that others are too.
- Believing that because *you* have come up with a solution you are so passionate about that others will want to buy it.
- Believing that *enough people* will want to buy it that you can make a business out of it.

This may sound like a counter-argument to being able to go where others can't and produce a better solution than anyone else because you are so passionate. So, it has to be balanced with a healthy dose of ensuring you use your passion as a superpower. And ensuring you use your passion to solve problems better because of your unique insight, and not by getting so caught up in believing you are right.

Add to this that passions are often so deeply personal, it's too easy to become offended or insulted when others don't share your level of enthusiasm.

Christopher Goodfellow – Box 2 Media

My partner told me he wanted to quit about a year after we started the business. It was horrible and looked like the whole thing would go under. Lucy-Rose told me taking the emotions out of business decisions was the hardest thing. It was like a penny-drop moment. I realized that so much of what I was looking for from the buy-out and the way the discussion was happening was tied up in my frustration and anger. When we acknowledged that, we were able to come to a sensible conclusion, the business continues to thrive and, best of all, we're still friends.

Chris was so passionate he couldn't understand why his business partner didn't share this. This is no reason to give up: it just serves as a great reminder that he needed to take the emotion out of his thought process for a moment as it was blinding his decision-making process. The trick is to be passionate about finding the best outcome, not about your first or only idea.

If your business does need support, partners, funding or even investment, then yes passion can be that great catalyst to get people excited in the first instance, but if you want their involvement in the long term then the kind of passion that will make a difference to your business is the passion to back this up with a sound business opportunity that they can invest in. You are not Kevin Costner and sadly this is not a case of 'build it and they will come'.

It doesn't prevent burnout

Just because working on your passion doesn't feel like work, it doesn't mean you won't get tired. The likelihood is you will work more hours and it will consume your thoughts night and day, and this is going to take an emotional toll on you – even when you love it.

We'll discuss in more depth in Chapter 5 about finding a balance between working hard and making progress, but we would be remiss not to mention an emerging trend and the slightly darker side of living the proverbial entrepreneurial dream – the media portrayal of what an entrepreneur should look like, how you should act, and the personal sacrifices that you have to make to be successful.

The mental health impact of the continued hustle and grind culture is increasingly being reported by entrepreneurs around the world. A recent survey by the International Business

Festival[8] found that most entrepreneurs struggle to switch off from the 'always on' working culture of today with more than half of business owners staying at work past 10pm, and a similar proportion sending work emails after midnight. You might be an early bird or a night owl, but you can't be both seven days a week.

Nick Elston – Forging People

I was keeping my anxiety in, not sharing it, and after a breakdown I decided to share my story. It was as a hobby, a passion at first. I started doing speaking events and telling my story regularly. Then I had to make a call to give up my job and started speaking full time. I liked the idea of being self-employed although that all changes when you leave the shores of employment.

Speaking as a job is fairly irregular and when you're speaking without an upsell, you're a one-hit wonder. I was in passion mode, trying to help as many people as possible. There was all this free stuff and I just couldn't say no to people. The more I started doing this as my sole job, my mental health started to decline as I wasn't looking after myself.

I was doing four events a week, tapping into my emotion on every occasion, so I was completely wiped, and the business model was flawed. I got to a few months in and then I took a part-time delivery job with Tesco to keep the money coming in. I started to question everything; has this gone too far or in an ideal world what does this look like?

---

[8] Charlie Mullins (8 May 2018), 'Being driven and focused is a blessing, but entrepreneurs need to learn to switch off', *Real Business*. Available from: https://realbusiness.co.uk/being-driven-is-blessing-but-entrepreneurs-should-learn-to-switch-off/ [accessed November 2019].

I wanted to speak twice a week and pay the mortgage, so I started to develop a business around that. Now I'm focusing on my ethics, but it's taken the form of a business, so it's not so emotionally invested.

Passion will not do anything to prevent this, and in Nick's case it was even exacerbating the condition. You do not need to suffer for your cause. I'm here now to give you permission to stop, and to tell you it's perfectly normal to get tired or to get excited about taking a break or having a holiday. No one is going to judge you, or at least no one who matters anyway. And anyone worth their salt understands that the better care you take of yourself, the better you are going to be able to serve what you are passionate about anyway. In fact, if you think about it this way, you're doing your passion a disservice by subscribing to the hustle and grind nonsense.

The kind of passion that will make a difference to your business is *not* the kind of passion that is defined by sacrifice and guilt or working until you burn out. It *is* defined by a better and happier life for everyone, including you. Go on, give yourself permission not to passionately work yourself into the ground.

The big f**k you

For some of us, it's possible to mistake being driven to prove people wrong for a passion to build your business. Are you really passionate about the business, or are you just hungry for the challenge to show that you can create something others thought you weren't capable of? If it works, great, but all too often it can easily go the other way.

Luke Johnson shares how he has thrived on this approach his whole life.

I'm a great guitarist and I've got a good ear. At school my teacher would give me a piece of music and say: 'This is hard, you could probably play it in a year.' My reaction was always to think: 'F**k you I can do that in a week.' It was a challenge because someone said I couldn't do it and I could; I loved that.

As an entrepreneur I still want to prove people wrong when they tell me I can't achieve something. I love it. Tell me 'I can't'; I am going to get it done. The happiest I have been in this business recently is when I've made the decision to change direction even when things have been going smoothly. Something inside me says 'f*ck it; it's probably not going to work' but what drives me is creating new opportunities and proving people wrong that say it won't work. That's the fun. I would get sick of it if we are having too much success. I would get bored if it was comfortable.

Luke's story isn't uncommon and what's important here is to tune in to what bit of building a business you are actually passionate about. For Luke, the passion wasn't about this business, or the previous one or the one before that. He had a desire in his life to prove something to himself and other people, to challenge himself in that way, and he wasn't satisfied if he wasn't doing that. Sometimes this led to unnecessary self-destruction along the way so that he had something to rebuild and start the cycle all over again.

If this is resonating at all, then ultimately your passion is misguided and is not going to be the kind that is going to support the best interests of your business. If you think you are in this position, then it might be time for someone else to take the reins and let you move on to your next challenge.

The right kind of passion

I don't believe that you can ever have too much passion. It's about understanding what passion is and how you can use it as a force for good in your business. Let's call it entrepreneurial passion rather than regular passion simply because I don't think regular passion quite does you justice. And here's my definition of entrepreneurial passion. *Entrepreneurial passion* is:

- The kind that gets you out of bed in the morning more than anything else does, because you simply can't bear to waste a minute doing anything else.
- The kind of passion that gets you through the tough times instead of giving up.
- The kind of passion that drives you to stay curious, creative, innovative and seek new solutions to problems over and over again; the kind where you go beyond your comfort zone to understand the real root of customer problems and address them. And the kind where you are blinded by your assumptions that because you are passionate you already know the answer.
- The kind of passion that recognizes when to engage your heart, and when to engage your head for the greater good of your business and your customer.
- The kind of passion that gets people excited in the first instance, and then backs it up with a sound business opportunity that supporters can invest in.
- The kind of passion that *is* defined by a better and happier life for everyone, including you. *Not* the kind of passion that is defined by sacrifice and guilt or working until you burn out.
- The kind of passion to find your purpose in life and follow it, not just a desire to prove others wrong or do something because someone said it couldn't be done.

It is *this* kind of passion that I believe is the reason that, when asked, the majority of people say that passion is the key to be a successful entrepreneur, yet it is so often undersold. Looking at that list I know that is the kind of passion I have for completing this book. Can you say you have that kind of passion for your business?

Course correction questions

- Look at the definition of entrepreneurial passion – is it you? Could you put your hand on your heart and say that you are displaying all of this?
- When did you last question your business model? Are you blind to flaws in your plans because more than anything you want it to work, rather than knowing for sure it can?
- What does burnout look like for you and are you close to it in the belief that it's the only way to display your passion?

What do you need to... Stop, Start and Continue doing now?

STOP

- Doing things that don't get you leaping out of bed in the morning and find something that does

- Using passion to describe everything you're enthusiastic about

- Being a slave and burning yourself out unnecessarily

- Believing that just because you're passionate you are right. And recognize that it can make you blind to possible flaws

START

- Figuring out when to use your heart and when to use your head to guide the direction of your passion for maximum impact

- ⊕ Doing your best work, not your hardest

- ⊕ Finding an enjoyable hard – the kind of challenges you thrive in, not the kind that cause you to self-destruct

CONTINUE

- ⊕ Being passionate! But not the boring ordinary kind – being entrepreneurially passionate – the remarkable kind

- ⊕ Doing the things that you *can't not* do

- ⊕ Being infectious with the things you are truly passionate about

Bonus exercise: The blinded by passion test

When it comes to being passionate, one of the areas that we covered in this chapter that can really trip us up is when passion can prevent us from seeing our business through the eyes of the customer and being blind to any potential flaws. Just because we are passionate doesn't mean we're right.

To make sure you don't fall into the trap of being blinded by passion, you can test yourself regularly to make sure you're working on insight and fact rather than assumptions based on your own feelings and perceptions.

Q. What did most people really tell you was their problem? Give yourself an honest rating.

You are not your customer – Lots of business ideas start with a personal pain point. An entrepreneur will encounter something that ticks them off and sets out on a quest to solve that problem for everyone. Are you being honest with yourself about whether or not other people share that pain point? Have you really been listening or only looking for the ones that do?

Q. How many customers have you asked that don't know you and won't be worried about hurting your feelings? Be honest.

You are in love with your idea – You cherish your idea and want everyone to think it's wonderful. You know who won't tell you it has flaws? Your friends and family. Your mum is not likely to crush your dreams by telling you it's rubbish and no one will buy it.

Q. How many customers have you identified that sincerely need what you have to offer?

Just because you can, doesn't mean you should – There are ideas, and then there are ideas that solve genuine problems that exist for customers. Don't be so excited by your idea that you fail to realize that no need for it exists.

Q. How are they currently solving their problems and what makes your solution so special? Score yourself against the competition.

You believe your customers will never change – Remember Kodak? Blockbuster? HMV? All victims of not adapting to changing customer habits. Doing this test is not a one-off exercise; it should be constant whatever the age and size of your business. Go deep, go broad and go often.

Q. Can you describe your exact customer persona in detail, or are you generalizing? How do you know?

You believe your customers all look the same – The more customers you speak to, the more you will realize that they describe their problems in different ways. They have slightly different preferences and lifestyles. They engage with different media and want different things from products.

Q. How often do you do this?

This test is supposed to be hard, and you might not like some of the answers – I'm sure you would much rather just get on with building your business. But if you skip it, you're effectively tossing a coin with the next few years of your life. Is that a risk you want to take?

4

Misadventures in...

SACRIFICE AND GUILT

We know that your passion can become all-consuming, particularly when you are also striving all the time to make a living from it. It can be easy to find yourself out of balance in other areas of your life.

Lucy-Rose and I normally try to purposely stay away from using the phrase work/life balance because we don't really believe it exists. And before you do a backflip, this is not about promoting the idea that we'll become workaholics, we'll burn out or our mental health will suffer. Let me explain – most people who are searching for work/life balance are actually desperately seeking a world where they feel less guilty about how they spend their time.

Don't believe me? Tell me what you were looking for when you decided that being an entrepreneur would give you a better work/life balance?

- Spend more time with the kids = feeling guilty for spending so much time at work
- Spend more time with your partner/spouse = feeling guilty for spending so much time at work

⦿ Spend more time at the gym = feeling guilty for spending so much time doing anything but the things that will make you fit

At Entrepreneurial Spark we saw many people start a business with the intention of being able to live life on their own terms. This might be you right now? Perhaps you thought that when you started your business it would give you more time to spend with the kids, or more flexibility to do some of the other stuff that you weren't able to do when you had a job, like walk the dog and go to the gym?

But here you are a few weeks, months or years down the track and things haven't quite worked out like that. You're still saying stuff to yourself (or your family and friends) like: 'Ah but it's OK because when we get over this hump/deliver this next product/secure that next client/hire that new staff member/ finish that campaign (delete as appropriate) it will all be better and we can be "normal" again.' And how many times during this adventure have you been able to be normal, or normal in the way you remember or envisaged when you first thought that having your own business was going to be able to give you a good 'work/life balance'?

And how many times have you felt even more guilty because nothing has really changed?

Getting started in business is a fantastic never-ending cycle of not having enough money to hire anyone and having to be every person that the business needs, simultaneously coupled with having neither the skills nor the hours in the day to be all of those people. That means you have to do everything and juggle all your life priorities too. As Emma describes here, there is only one of you and you can't split yourself into a thousand pieces on a daily basis.

Emma Baylin – Shared Harmonies

> *It is really difficult when you are trying to be a sole entrepreneur, a sole parent and a sole me, and trying to be the best one of each all the time is almost an impossible task. But each one is really valid and important. What's most important is trying to get the strategies in place to keep each one as equitable as possible and just keeping an eye on when they're not and trying to redress that balance...*

> *As an entrepreneur you don't work a nine to five or even a regular rhythm. I assumed other people were more organized than I was, but even people that book me will ring at the last minute and my week can turn on a sixpence. Then I have to make those calculated/really hard choices to miss out on something for the business because I have to step back into the space of being a mum, or in reverse when I know my son needs me but I can't miss the opportunity for the business.*

What about if we created a life where we spent less time feeling guilty and spent more time doing the things that we don't have to feel guilty about?

Sounds idyllic, right?

When you are an entrepreneur there really is no such thing as a big dividing line between life and work. It's not a black and white thing: you don't have work things and life things. It's about your work being an integral part of a whole life that you choose to create for yourself.

It just becomes part of you and what you do – your purpose, your values and doing the things you love every day – and you have to give it your whole self. This life isn't just about showing up from Monday to Friday between nine and five pm; it's not a job title. Being an entrepreneur is about who you are for all 24 hours of the day and it shouldn't be filled with things you feel guilty about.

It's entirely up to *you* to create that life that you don't have to feel guilty about.

Guilt and sacrifice

The thing about guilt is that it makes doing the things we want to do feel like sacrifices, when in the end they are just decisions based on what seems right to us at the time. This isn't an easy process because we don't always know what we really want and sometimes we discover that we've allowed ourselves to prioritize something that shouldn't have been that high on the list. We've spun one plate at the expense of another plate that was really important to us. It's a learning process that we have to go through and sometimes it's not an easy one.

Most of the time it means a continuous process of redefining the idea of what balance means to you as an individual. It might include redefining working convention, or working hours, working days and even working clothes. It also sometimes means realizing when making your daughter a cake takes precedence over building global communities. Or doing something that you know is going to be beneficial to you but feeling guilty because it doesn't meet what we believe to be the criteria of 'doing work'. Going to the gym isn't working. Walking the dog isn't working. Taking a day off isn't working. Or is it?

Kerry Harrison – Tiny Giant

I had to get buy-in from my husband to do this, not that he decides for us like that, but it needed to be a family decision, or I knew it was going to be too hard work. He says things like, 'Oh its fine for you to go off and seek your passion while I work nine to five in the office', and I sometimes feel really guilty about that. But at the same time, I do need to have that to allow me to do it because if he was freelance and I was freelance I think it would be a really unstable environment to bring our children up in.

So, he has been really supportive, and he does get a bit frustrated because the thing about being an entrepreneur and working for yourself (and maybe I should be a bit more disciplined about this) is that you just work all the time. I work in the evenings, I work in the days, people email me at weekends, I have conversations at weekends, I record podcasts at weekends, I draft someone an email on a Sunday and people get back to me on a Sunday afternoon at like 2pm and I think wow this is just such a different world.

And he gets frustrated with me because he says, 'I haven't seen you', and we do have arguments about pulling our weight with the kids, but in general he is really supportive and if I have a bad day, he is also really good. He's really proud of where I've got to and I genuinely think it's really important to have someone like that on your side.

I haven't found a balance; maybe it's the early days, but I see most people working ridiculously long hours and it feels like this is almost part of being an entrepreneur. I think in time I will try and be a bit more disciplined. I do still try to run, I do quite a bit of running and I do try and make sure that I still do that because I know if I don't, I feel quite grumpy. And I also make sure that I put the children to bed and read them a story as well as trying to spend time with them at the weekend – but I don't feel like I've got the balance quite right yet.

The real balancing act you are going to have to master is figuring out what you should and shouldn't feel guilty about. And to do that you need to be clear about your priorities, and then use them to guide you when you're fighting with the urge to do something else.

Focus on the things that matter that day and do your best. If the priorities have to change the next day because you recognize that you should have focused on something else, then that's OK too.

Asking yourself some questions about how you feel can be useful. Things like:

- Do the rewards I will get from focusing on this outweigh the sacrifices I will have to make today?
- Does the pride I feel in my achievement in the long term outweigh the guilt I feel over the compromises I have had to/will have to make?
- Will this make me feel genuinely fulfilled or does it just feel like more of a grind?
- Is this something I really want to do or am I doing it because I feel that it's expected of me by someone else – be it my partner, my colleague, my family, my friends, my peers, or society as a whole?

Sometimes you will have to choose short-term sacrifice for a long-term reward – in the end, it's your choice and what is right for you won't be right for the next person.

Prioritizing

Knowing what to prioritize can be a real dilemma and can end up feeling as though you either pick one thing to focus on and sacrifice all the rest or feel guilty for picking one thing and try to split yourself across everything.

A few years ago, *Inc. Magazine* published an article featuring Randy Zuckerberg on 'the entrepreneur's dilemma', where she had another idea. She summed up the idea of balance as an entrepreneur in one tweet:

> *Work, sleep, family, fitness or friends: Pick 3.*[9]

That 48-character tweet is now a whole book[10] and the idea is still as simple – we can't give every aspect of our full self all of the time. It's a lose-lose situation where we'd just be dividing ourselves into too many parts and not giving any aspect the kind of attention it deserves. And choosing an area of focus doesn't have to be a permanent state either. We don't have to pick three for life and feel guilty about the rest, *we just have to pick three for today.*

Try this one out loud:

> *'I don't have to figure it all out today. I just have to pick the three things I need to give my full attention to today and then I can reassess it all again tomorrow.'*

Now, consciously pick the three (or fewer if you like) things you are going to focus on *guilt free* for today. Go on, try it.

The three things I am going to focus on *guilt free* for today are:

1. _____

2. _____

3. _____

---

[9] Jessica Stillman (February 2016), 'Work, sleep, family, fitness, or friends: Pick 3', *Inc.* Available from: www.inc.com/jessica-stillman/work-sleep-family-fitness-or-friends-pick-3.html [accessed May 2019].
[10] Randi Zuckerberg (2018), *Pick Three*, Dey Street Books.

If you are still struggling, then I would suggest you go back and tap into your vision and values exercise to guide you here. If you were being true to that vision and those values, what would you be doing today?

Remember you are not choosing for life, just today.

Saying no

Are you one of those people that everyone can rely on? The person that says yes to looking after the neighbour's cat even though you don't really want to. Do you hold the business together, making sure everyone else has everything they need when they need it? Are you the one everyone calls on when they need help because they know you'll drop everything and do it? Do you plug all of the leaks and take on the stress for everyone around you, leaving little for yourself? And when you do give yourself a little time and attention you feel guilty about it?

Let's talk about the N word. That tiny, simple, powerful, yet oh so difficult to say word. No.

One of the underlying reasons why you might be feeling overwhelmed or being pulled in many different directions is because you haven't said 'no' to enough things lately. If you were to look back at your last week, would you say that you have been 'too busy'? I'm going to guess the answer is yes, because as an entrepreneur it's always yes. Who has the luxury of not being busy?

Here's a more telling question, what were you busy doing? Busy mercilessly progressing your business?

We can all be held accountable for being busy at times. When it comes down to it and you ask yourself honestly, are you saying yes to things when you should really be saying no? Are you feeling guilty because you have let unimportant tasks take priority over the things you know you should be doing?

If that's the case, you're not alone.

At Entrepreneurial Spark, Lucy-Rose developed the nickname the Smiling Assassin because she was the absolute queen at being able to say no with a smile on her face. She took it as a compliment. She was ruthless in her focus because she realized that she could never hope to achieve her larger goals if she didn't take control, prioritize herself and learn to say no in a positive way. As we scaled our business, she was always mindful of time being the one thing you can never get back.

So, what stops most of us from being able to say no often enough?

Firstly, we can be overly polite. Most of us have no idea how to say no and so we believe that we will be offending people if we do. That leads us to saying yes even though we're screaming 'no' in our heads. And the worst bit is we feel obliged to give an elaborate reason why.

Another favourite that stops us from saying no is our instant gratification monkey.[11] That's the part of our brain that takes over when we see new and shiny things and persuades us that we'd be much happier doing this than what we're doing right now. Particularly if what we're doing now is hard, and our instant gratification monkey is already subconsciously on the lookout for a way to sabotage us.

---

[11] Tim Urban (2016), 'Inside the mind of a master procrastinator'. Available from: www.ted.com/talks/tim_urban_inside_the_mind_of_a_master_procrastinator?language=enTED / YouTube [accessed June 2018].

And then there's FOMO as the cool kids term it, or Fear of Missing Out. What if we choose to prioritize our three things today and we accidentally miss out on 16 other new and exciting opportunities because we were laser focused? What if…?!?

We have so many techniques we use to say yes when we really should be saying no, it's about time we worked on our techniques for saying no. So, I picked the brains of the Smiling Assassin and here are her top tips for prioritizing you and your goals and not feeling guilty for saying no to other people.

1. Give yourself permission to politely say no and mean it. So often, we don't feel comfortable saying no so what we actually end up saying is 'maybe'. All we're doing here is creating an infinite cycle of not wanting to do the thing that we have now partially committed ourselves to and then torturing ourselves trying to find a way to let people down gently, when what we should have done is politely decline in the first place.

2. Apply the 80/20 rule.[12] That is that 80% of your outcomes, advances or opportunities come from 20% of your inputs or interactions. Or in other words, prioritize the big wins. Assess every opportunity that comes your way and decide what value it will add and then make a call on how much time or resource you allocate to it. Take the time to ask the question: 'How does this help me achieve my vision?'

3. Don't waste time. If a potentially great opportunity does present itself, ask yourself does this really require an hour-long meeting? Or would a short call work to assess the situation, get all the facts and build the relationship you need? Everyone comes out feeling happy as you have

---

[12] Carla Tardi (2020), '80-20 rule', *Investopedia*. Available from: www.investopedia.com/terms/1/80-20-rule.asp [accessed February 2020].

discussed it and you have next steps. If the outcome is that you don't proceed, people will respect you more if you don't waste their time with lengthy calls or meetings that you know aren't going anywhere.

4. Be disciplined with your time and energy while still nurturing and enjoying important relationships. Lucy-Rose has a reputation for doing this with her friends. If she knows she's going to Edinburgh (where she used to live), she's been known to schedule to meet three friends back to back. She says: 'In the time I am with them I am in the moment and we have a great time; we both leave feeling good.'
   While this makes me feel a bit cringey, there is a level of discipline there that I can only dream of aspiring to! I can also think of plenty of other scenarios where I could apply this logic.

5. Prioritize, prioritize, prioritize. Instead of writing endless to-do lists, use the same 'pick three' discipline, apply it to your daily task list and don't let anything stand in the way of achieving them. You will feel a much greater sense of satisfaction than drowning on a daily basis.

6. If you're thinking the last point is unachievable because as an entrepreneur, we always have to stay flexible and adaptable to change then you would be right. So, Lucy-Rose's next tip is don't fill every minute of every day with meetings or calls. Don't wake up on Monday morning with 10 scheduled back to back. Life throws us curveballs, so schedule in admin or thinking time every week. It will make you more productive in the long run. If someone sends you an invite for a meeting at that precious time, it's OK to press the decline button.

Saying no is not always easy but try implementing these six tips and you'll be amazed at how much more you can achieve and how much better you're going to feel.

Forgiveness

I realize all of this is easy to say and not as easy to do. Having what feels like so much to do in so little time can be overwhelming. You aren't always going to get this right, and it's going to be a struggle. At times *everything* is going to seem as though it's the right thing to be doing and you're going to have a hard time saying no. You will need to find strategies to help you determine what's right, right now and what's right in the long run.

This might become the ultimate test of your values and whether you've got them right if you find that you actually have two in conflict and your gut is telling you to prioritize one over the other. Remember this is a process of learning and helping you become more aware of yourself and how you make decisions. You can't and won't get it right first or every time.

As hard as it is to hear, you won't plug all the leaks, you won't whack all the moles, and you will drop some of the spinning plates in the process and that's OK. It's all part of being human and it's all part of learning to figure out your unique way of entrepreneuring.

When this happens, you really have to practise being kind to yourself. Because, unless you are a sociopath, then consciously or subconsciously you need to believe that you are always trying to do the right thing. No one intentionally makes a poor decision or takes their eye off the ball, so if you do somehow drop a plate then you can't dwell on it or beat yourself up for it. Know that this is hard, and you won't always make the right decision. And if you're using Randi Zuckerberg's method of only picking three for today – it was *only for today*. Cut yourself some slack and try again tomorrow. If it felt good at the time, you have nothing to apologize or feel guilty for.

A cautionary tale of sacrifice and guilt

This is my own cautionary tale about the sacrifices I made when I first became an entrepreneur. I'm opening up this story here because I know I am not the only one who will have found myself in this position of not recognizing before it was too late when my sacrifices had gone too far and left me with guilt that I found very difficult to shake.

When I first began my adventure into entrepreneuring, I was happily married. I worked hard and challenged myself and I thought I had achieved quite a lot in my life. Then I discovered a kind of work that would completely surpass any previous experience of work that I had ever had – it was addictive.

I suddenly found myself in a place where I just got it: this purpose thing everyone was talking about. I loved going to work and I loved working with entrepreneurs. And yes, I was stretched beyond my comfort zone daily, but I thought about work and the entrepreneurs all the time, at evenings, weekends and even on holidays. I was so inspired by the kinds of people I was working with that I couldn't not be compelled to support them in their endeavours.

I've always thought that eating, sleeping and breathing something was an odd turn of phrase but I was definitely in that place. I was working long hours, I was taking my work home with me, on holiday with me, talking about it at the dinner table – it was all I could focus on. Inevitably it started to have an impact on my relationship.

My husband didn't understand, and on reflection most likely because I didn't help him to understand. Not intentionally, but simply because I had never experienced the feeling before and I don't think I understood it myself. I never knew this kind of personal development existed and now I could see what I had been missing. All I allowed my husband to see was that I was spending more and more time 'working'.

I was like a superhero/supervillain discovering my powers for the first time and misfiring in all directions. I wasn't in tune with myself or in control of my emotions and I didn't really understand where I was going with it. The reward for me was that I was growing, discovering new things about myself and I was loving it – when in fact my husband and I were growing further apart without me noticing.

My husband began to feel like he was playing second fiddle and resenting me for spending all my time working. This turned to me resenting him for trying to drag me away from the thing that I had grown to love doing. It was a vicious downward spiral for about two years and eventually our marriage didn't survive. Looking back, I'm not proud of how that situation turned out or my part in it. If anyone has ever been in a marriage breakdown situation, it's not fun for anyone and I ask myself often whether or not things could have been different or if I could have made better decisions.

My conclusion is that yes, I absolutely could. I was focused on the daily gratification that I was getting from work and I was sacrificing my personal relationship. That would have been a tolerable balance for days at a time, but not for months or two years as it turned out. I wasn't checking in on what was important each day or redressing the balance, and on reflection there were many reasons for that.

My cautionary tale to you is to make sure you look up regularly and check in – with yourself, your partner, your co-founder or any of the other important people in your life who are on this ride with you. Many years later, I still feel mixed emotions about it. It has most definitely been one of life's greatest teachers and reminds me every day to think about what sacrifices are for today, and what are for the long term.

Course correction questions

- Ask yourself honestly – what is causing you to feel guilty right now and why?
- Have you gone too far and prioritized one area too much? If so, how can you redress the balance?
- Are you saying yes to things that aren't getting you anywhere? What do you need to learn to say no to?

What do you need to... Stop, Start and Continue doing now?

STOP

- Kidding yourself that somehow 'balance' will come – you have to create your own version of balance
- Living a life that you feel guilty about
- Beating yourself up for sometimes getting your priorities wrong and dropping a ball here and there

START

- Creating a life you don't need to feel guilty for by consciously choosing where to spend your time today
- Picking one to three focus areas each day, then re-evaluating the next day
- Choosing what is important to you the most, based on your vision and values – remembering to include your whole life in your vision, not just your business
- Saying no guilt free to things that don't serve you

CONTINUE

- Reprioritizing – daily

- Forgiving yourself for not getting it right all the time – you might never get it right!

Bonus exercise: Practise prioritizing and saying no

Try this.

Reflecting back on a week where you felt overwhelmed, guilty and as though you were making too many sacrifices (and without kicking yourself):

- How were your energy levels?
- Did you achieve everything you wanted to?
- If not, why not? What got in the way?
- Of the things that got in the way, what could you have said no to in hindsight?

Looking forward to today, or tomorrow:

- What do you need to prioritize your energy for?
- What effect will taking on new and unexpected tasks or responsibilities have on that energy?
- If something comes up that doesn't fit with your priorities, how can you comfortably say no to it without feeling guilty?
- How can you practise this so you're ready for it when it happens?

5

Misadventures in...

FINDING BALANCE

We've already established that we don't believe in work/life balance as a concept because on most occasions when people use the term, it's normally to refer to a situation where they feel guilty for spending time doing something they love instead of what they feel they should be doing, or the other way around.

But what happens when it feels like there still aren't enough hours in the day to attend to everything you want to do? In this chapter we're going to talk about what happens when you're torn between something you love and something else you love.

It's a balancing act that's even harder to get right and one that you will feel like you ride a tightrope between regularly. Let's see if you recognize any of these balancing acts you are going to have to overcome on a daily basis:

1. Providing for you and your family versus spending time with your family (and friends).
2. Creating more hours in the day versus getting enough sleep.
3. Working hard versus working smart.
4. Convenience and getting stuff done versus diet and exercise.

Finding balance isn't about having the perfect proportion of time set aside in the day for each thing. It's about balancing your mental and physical energy and emotions to enable you to do all the things you want to do and not sacrifice yourself, your health or your relationships in the process.

Providing for you and your family versus spending time with your family (and friends)

I don't think this one needs much explanation. If you are an entrepreneur who has a family, or friends, or both – then you'll get this one. You love your family and you desperately want to spend time with them but at the same time you feel an obligation to keep them safe, put a roof over their head and put food on the table.

You spend your days going back and forth between trying to get home for dinner and getting that last job out of the door, so you know that you're going to have income the next month. You find yourself between earning enough to go on a family holiday but not being able to relax for a minute because you're worrying about being away from the business.

> *Victoria Green of Victoria Green Ltd found herself on the phone to her Chinese supplier just minutes before her son's school nativity play because they had questions about her order for 60,000 units for a major department store – unless she wants to lose the order she has to take the call.*

> *Matt Kandela of Dear Future who loves his wife and one year old daughter more than life itself, but sometimes (and only sometimes) is pleased (and feels mildly guilty) when they find something to do without him on a Saturday and he can enjoy a day of quiet working while everyone else is enjoying their weekends.*

My uncle is an entrepreneur. He works too hard, or too much, or something along these lines, according to most members of our family. When I spoke to my cousin recently about this constant battle that entrepreneurs have between their work and their family, we talked about her dad and her reflections on the time he spent working when she was younger. She admitted that it would have been lovely if he'd spent more time at home, or on holiday, or just with the family as a whole. But then she also acknowledged that without him providing for the family they couldn't have had a lot of the things they had. That's not to say that they were materialistic or anything, but his contribution meant things like a university education, a reasonable standard of living and a nice house.

I challenged her with the question that if you know that your family desperately need and want to spend more time with you, then why wouldn't you just pull back a little and swing the balance in the opposite direction? Isn't it a bit selfish to keep working so hard? Well, my cousin said: 'He also really loves what he does – is it more selfish to ask him to give that up?' When I thought that one through, I had to admit that I hadn't thought about the side of the debate where it's good for kids to see a parent being fulfilled by their work and it being a positive and enjoyable part of life. I'd learned a new angle on the matter.

And it's such a fine line between what you want to do, what other people want you to do, and what you feel like you 'should' be doing. In the end, it only really comes down to the impact it has on you and the impact it has on the people you love the most. If the balance continues to swing in the direction of a negative impact on you or your loved ones, then there's no doubt that someone is going to start to feel a bit crap.

Even when we think we're devoting time to friends and family, it can often feel like such a challenge. Are you answering emails under the table when you are out with your other half for a 'nice dinner'? Or my personal favourite – pretending you need to go to the toilet and taking your phone (needs must) so you can respond to calls, texts or check your social media.

I've shamelessly stolen the following from an Instagram post from Mel Bound of This Mum Runs. Mel is an entrepreneur we worked with in Bristol and this is a post about a picture of a chocolate owl cake she had made that morning:

My 8 year old does not care that I've had the craziest of weeks in the investment raising circus…

It's her birthday and a chocolate owl cake was top of the list, tired Mama or not. Tempting as it was to outsource or head to Sainsbury's, making this cake is how I spent my morning ahead of an afternoon of 15 kids and some giant inflatables at her swimming party.

Juggling a growing business and a young family is not for the faint hearted. My son was 10 months old when I started @thismumruns and man it's been tough to get the balance right, mostly I get it wrong.

But today I made this cake. And I dedicate it to all you mums and dads with businesses out there. I see you, I hear you, I feel the millions of plates you have in the air. This cake is for you my friends.

#working #parents #entrepreneur #family #balance #platespinning #startuplife

At that moment in time, Mel's daughter needed her to make a cake. It wasn't glamorous; it wasn't all about investor conversations and pitch decks and bringing the next raise into the business. It was probably messy and sticky and with more chocolate on hands and faces than on the cake. And if Mel was honest with herself, it was probably the best kind of relief that she needed from the investment circus of a week. Mel doesn't claim to have balance, just to be doing her best to give herself time and energy where and when it's needed.

It just so happens for Mel that her customers are people just like her – mums trying to find a way to make work more flexible – and that dropping work for a few hours making cake is exactly the thing that is going to keep Mel connected with the needs of her customers. It's not working life; it's real life, and it's a daily choice.

There is no prescription that I can give you in this book that says when you have to prioritize one over the other. But when it comes to balancing out these sides of the coin, it's going to be essential to allow your heart and your head to work together. And be present when you need to be. You and everyone you love deserve the best version of you, not the one that wishes they were elsewhere.

Creating more hours in the day versus getting enough sleep

When time is your most valuable commodity and you've 'got too much to do', sleep is normally the first thing to get the chop. You're juggling priorities and you don't want to let anyone else down so instead you gain yourself a couple of hours a day by shaving that off the number of hours you sleep. Nice idea?

I used to think Arnold Schwarzenegger had the answer to how much sleep we really need as entrepreneurs. I am a huge Arnold fan, not because of his startling performance in *Conan the Barbarian* or because I think he'll ever win an Oscar for his acting prowess,[13] but because of his general attitude to life.

In Arnold's six rules for success he says:

> *If you want to win, there is absolutely no way around hard, hard work. None of my rules, by the way, of success, will work unless you do. I've always figured out that there are 24 hours a day. You sleep six hours and have 18 hours left. Now, I know there are some of you out there that say well, wait a minute, I sleep eight hours or nine hours. Well, then, just sleep faster, I would recommend.*[14]

Sleep faster! Genius. And I find it hard to argue with a seven-time Mr. Olympia, Hollywood legend and two-term Governor of California. And one who decided to start body building at age 15 so he could win Mr. Olympia because he believed that this was his path to moving from Second World War torn Austria to the US to become a Hollywood actor like his hero Reg Park. But… in this instance, I'm going to have to disagree with his prescription of six hours sleep a night and his recommendation to 'sleep faster'.

This is partly because I've just read *Why We Sleep* by Matthew Walker and I'm completely blown away by all of the newly discovered benefits of sleep, and partly because I know what a wreck you can be or how ineffective you can be when you don't get enough sleep. Like 'hangry', but about sleep instead

---

[13] Despite 'I'll be back' making it to #37 in the American Film Institute list of 100 movie quotes of all time…

[14] Arnold Schwarzenegger (2009), '6 rules for success', *Graduation Wisdom*. Available from: www.graduationwisdom.com/speeches/0067-schwarzenegger.htm [accessed June 2018].

of food. Science dictates that sacrificing sleep just isn't good enough – our bodies and our brains are too precious to deprive ourselves of sleep (and if you don't believe me then just read the book[15]). Matthew goes on to describe the practice as 'self-euthanasia'.

So, pulling that all-nighter, or staying up late to answer those last emails just doesn't work for most people in the long term. Also, if you've ever woken up to a barrage of 11pm emails from a colleague the night before, it's not big and it's not clever and you're not impressing anyone – don't be that person.

Yes, we've all been there, and we've all gone without sleep to get us through a tough patch. Late nights, early mornings, deadlines, spinning all of those plates and pretending to the outside world that we've got all of this under control. Sometimes it is necessary to get a job done, to make sure you are one step ahead. You also might be one of these people who functions well at night or early in the morning and you should definitely capitalize on your most productive hours of the day; just make sure you get some sleep at either end.

What I'm saying is – don't be a martyr or a slave to the number of hours you work and the sleep you lose – it's not helpful and no one will thank you for it. You'll be tired, irritable and according to Matthew Walker your cognitive function can be up to 40% less effective than if you got a decent night's sleep. Not to mention the fact that it's proven you eat more if you're sleep deprived!

---

[15] In fact, I have had to stop reading *Why We Sleep* by Matthew Walker about two-thirds of the way through because I was becoming so anxious about not getting enough sleep and the detrimental effect it was having on me that it was becoming counter-productive and in fact I was beginning to *lose* sleep as a result!

Lucy-Rose and I have been referring to our Entrepreneurial Spark years as 'the fat years' and now I know why.

I always remember a colleague telling me about how he gets up at 5am each morning, reads for an hour, works out, has breakfast and is still at his desk before anyone else. I used to be in awe of this discipline and amazed at how someone could get up at 5am each morning and not be a total zombie... but then I never did ask what time he goes to bed. What works for one person won't necessarily work for others; you have to find your own rhythm.

This is one balancing act where the pendulum should not swing in favour of sacrificing sleep regularly. Sleep deprivation cannot be a permanent state to the detriment of our health. With every bout of serious hard work and sacrificial sleep must come a period of recovery and the time to feel proud of your achievements and enjoy the rewards of your labour. Let's try and also retain a few brain cells and some sanity while we're seeking some kind of balance.

Working hard versus working smart

As we described in Chapter 1, it has never been cooler or sexier to call yourself an entrepreneur. But as I am sure you are finding out, getting there is the exact opposite of sexy. The day-to-day effort that is required to achieve success is the opposite of cool, trendy or sexy. It's blooming hard work, and it's sweat.

So why do we do it? Because making new stuff, having new ideas, inspiring people, doing stuff you've never done before, achieving things you never thought possible, finding your purpose and doing what you love every day – that *is* exciting, appealing and very, very cool. And all of that stuff that feels hard becomes not so hard when it's something you genuinely love or believe in or want to spend your days doing.

So, let's be smart about this and let's not subscribe to the notion that we have to hustle and grind 24/7 to get to the place we want to get to. Let's make smart decisions about where to put our time and effort. By all means, aspire to be like your entrepreneuring idols but don't believe that you have to work 120 hours a week to get there. It's unlikely that is going to afford you a balanced and healthy life.

Just look at the Japanese. They have the highest productivity levels in the world coupled with the lowest happiness levels. The culture of hard work in Japan is driving young Japanese workers to 'karoshi' – the word the Japanese use for quite literally working themselves to death.[16]

Whenever we try to do something we haven't done before, there is going to be a degree of hard work involved. Let's be shrewd about when we have to work hard and not make this a permanent state either.

Around five years ago, I had the amazing opportunity to be at an event at US accelerator Mass Challenge in Boston where one of the speakers was Jeff Taylor, founder of Monster.com, a truly fascinating and inspiring speaker. He talked a lot about his start-up journey, how most of his ideas would come to him in the shower, and how this frustrated him greatly because it was too wet to write them down. In true entrepreneurial fashion, and much to his wife's delight, he invested in some waterproof

---

[16] Chris Weller (18 October 2017), 'Japan is facing a "death by overwork" problem – here's what it's all about', *Business Insider*. Available from: www.businessinsider.com/what-is-karoshi-japanese-word-for-death-by-overwork-2017-10?r=US&IR=T [accessed February 2019].

crayons and started drawing on the tiles in the bathroom while he was in the shower. You can imagine just how appealing his wife found that... shortly afterwards she confiscated his crayons.

After that, Jeff told us that he constantly carried a notebook around with him so that when he had ideas, he could quickly note them down and get back to what he was doing. The idea for Monster.com came to him in the middle of the night. He talks about reaching for his notebook at the side of the bed and starting to jot things down. When he couldn't switch off from it, he eventually had to get up and drive to a 24 hour coffee house, so he could keep sketching out his idea without waking anyone else in the house up.

This in itself isn't unusual for most people. Ideas don't work to a schedule; in fact, they generally arrive at the most inopportune moments. Ever tried to be 'deliberately creative'? It's difficult. For most of us it simply ends in a frustrating few minutes, hours or days staring at a blank piece of paper or computer screen.

What was unusual about Jeff Taylor was his attitude to balancing hard work and smart work. In the early days of building Monster.com, Jeff knew that the online recruitment market was ready to explode, so how was he going to stay ahead of the competition? He didn't know if his product was going to be bigger or better than anyone else's in those days, so the only thing he could do was make sure he got to market first.

Jeff proclaimed that every day he started work early in the morning and finished early in the evening and that suited him, except on one day a week. One day a week he would start at the normal time and work right through to the small hours of the following morning, putting in a 16 to 18 hour day. His reasoning was that each week he would have worked one day more than his competition. If he did that for a whole year, he could get to market 52 days ahead of them.

Now I don't subscribe in any way to the notion that hours worked alone equal success; I'm sure we all know a busy fool when we see one. And I'm definitely not prescribing less sleep – but in this case a temporary sacrifice certainly paid dividends for Jeff. Constant sleep deprivation was not a permanent sacrifice: just a once a week activity that he could recover quickly from but that made him (in his eyes) significant gains.

The internet is full of motivational quotes on what it takes to be successful. Like pro American footballer Jerry Rice:

> *'Do today what others won't so tomorrow you can have what others don't.'*

And while I believe that to be true, if sacrificing your physical and mental health becomes a permanent state then you're not going to be giving your business the best of you. Not to mention the damage to your long-term health.

For me, sacrifice means a sustained effort of substituting things in life in a way that others won't, but in a sustainable long-term way. And making sacrifices that others wouldn't, but in a way that you can still actually live – not the 24/7 hustle culture, as entrepreneur Mike Rucker Ph.D. describes it – the 'hustle porn' that the internet world believes we should be living.

> *For Gary Maitles of The Service Directory that meant selling his car and his bike and buying a £500 run-around to get to our accelerator every day in order to fund his business. And six years in, it still means going on the ferry to his holiday destination with his wife and while she watches Netflix on her tablet, he draws new wire frames for his website.*

Has he had some sleepless nights – of course. Has he had periods where he has had to make a deeper level of sacrifice – definitely. Is it still mentally challenging – absolutely. But on balance he's still healthy, his relationship is intact, and the business is still growing. After 24 months the business went from an idea with zero turnover, to employing two people with a seven-figure turnover. Now six years in and the company has four employees and turnover has grown consistently year on year since those first 24 months.

Don't mistake working hard for working smart and don't become a martyr. Learn to work smart so that you are mentally and physically able to put in the extra hard yards when it really counts, rather than needlessly running yourself into the ground on a constant basis.

Reframe your hours to suit you. Lucy-Rose is a morning person who likes to get the hard things off her plate early doors. I am an evening person. I prefer to get some exercise done in the morning to set myself up physically for the day and I prefer the calm of the evening when no one is calling or melting my inbox to get my best thought work done.

You only have one energy system and balance here is about making sure you charge and discharge at the times that are going to deliver the best results.

Convenience and getting stuff done versus diet and exercise

We all understand the notion that a healthy body equals a healthy mind. But why is it that diet and exercise are the first things to get sacrificed when we become busy?

You know that scenario well – you are 'too busy' or you 'don't have enough time' to go to the gym or to make yourself healthy food. You skip your workout and you pick up a sandwich from the filling station between meetings and eat it in the car. At the end of the day, you feel exhausted and crap. And you've probably wasted at least an hour of your day wishing you had time to exercise.

This is entirely fine for a day but add all those days up over the course of a year and you end up with a couple of extra pounds on and a car full of empty sandwich and crisp wrappers, and with each day you are becoming progressively more sluggish and unproductive. Let's also not forget that exercise gives you endorphins and a regular workout can do wonders for your mood.

'The fat years' as we referred to previously was a cycle that looked similar to the above except for Lucy-Rose and I most weeks were spent travelling around the UK opening accelerators. This meant Monday to Friday staying in hotels and taking planes, trains and automobiles to the four corners of the UK. It feels glamorous for a while but after you've seen your fifth airport or train station sandwich meal deal that week, or you've ended your night in the hotel bar having a gin to unwind for the third day running (or stocked up on a couple of 'train gins' for the journey…) and felt a bit foggy the next morning – then it all becomes a bit tiresome, your waistband starts complaining, and you're definitely not at your best or most productive.

It takes discipline to stay fit and healthy when the demands of your business are high. In our case it meant substituting the evening gin with taking our PE kit on our travels and getting up super early to get some sort of workout in. It took booking self-catering apartments instead of hotels so we could cook something healthier in the evening or eat a healthy breakfast. And it took going against all the trends and mentalities in business travel that involve going for drinks after work and making excuses for not maintaining some sort of routine.

Maybe you're the sort of person that skips breakfast and has a couple of strong coffees in the morning to get you fired up? Whether its yoga, lifting weights, going for a lunchtime walk, getting away from the desk, meditation, meal prep, walking the dog or just getting a good night's sleep, just remember the better care you take of your body and brain, the better it will perform for you in your business. And we haven't even mentioned carving out time for your own personal development yet – more on that in Chapter 8.

I know personally that I am a more productive person when I have exercised. Exercise is something I can do. It's something that I can achieve every day. I can win almost every day at exercise, so I don't just get a chemical rush that makes me more motivated; I get an ego boost as well.

There are so many healthy body = healthy mind reasons why I should prioritize getting 30–60 mins of exercise a day. It makes my life and work better, so I would be doing myself and my business a disservice if I didn't do it, not to mention the people that live with me. Like Kerry Harrison who feels a bit grumpy if she doesn't get her running in, what could you do tomorrow that you didn't do today that your body and brain will thank you for?

Course correction questions

- What change(s) could you make to achieve your own version of balance?
- How could you work smarter rather than harder?
- What one thing could you tweak to make your routine a bit healthier?

What do you need to... Stop, Start and Continue doing now?

STOP

- Sacrificing sleep or your health and wellbeing – it's a short-term gain for a long-term pain

- Misguidedly spreading yourself too thin

- Beating yourself up if you don't achieve anywhere near the right balance on any given day – you are trying and that's what matters

- Taking your family and friends for granted

START

- Choosing what is important to you the most – using your head and your heart to make decisions that require a joint approach

- Being present when you need to, not just showing up as a token gesture

- Charging and discharging your energy in places that need it most – not just working hard for the sake of it

- Checking in with your loved ones – again

CONTINUE

- ◉ Reprioritizing daily
- ◉ Fuelling your body with sources of energy that are going to help you to do more – healthy food, sleep, endorphins and exercise-related chemicals

---

Bonus exercise: Balancing the scales

Sometimes all you need to do to redress an imbalance in an area of your life is simply to recognize that the imbalance exists by understanding where you are today versus where you'd like to be. Then you can put a plan in place to get there.

Take each of the areas we've talked about in this chapter and give yourself a realistic assessment of where you are. Too far in one direction or just right? Don't forget that it's OK to experience short-term gains or make short-term sacrifices as long as the weight shifts back in the opposite direction again.

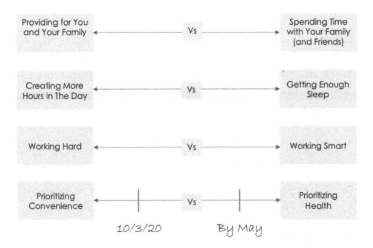

Providing for You and Your Family ←———— Vs ————→ Spending Time with Your Family (and Friends)

Creating More Hours in The Day ←———— Vs ————→ Getting Enough Sleep

Working Hard ←———— Vs ————→ Working Smart

Prioritizing Convenience ←——|—— Vs ——|——→ Prioritizing Health

10/3/20   *By May*

Try it now. Why not use one colour of pen to mark where you are now versus where you'd like to be? If you want to use your *Misadventures in Entrepreneuring Journal* you can add in additional notes on why you are where you are now and what steps you can put in place to get you closer to where you want to be.

6

Misadventures in...

KNOWING WHO YOUR CHAMPIONS ARE

It is a cliché as old as the hills to say that entrepreneuring is a lonely life. Yet one of the reasons Lucy-Rose and I began Misadventures in Entrepreneuring was because we spent a lot of the time wondering if we were the only ones going through all sorts of things we never expected.

The truth, as we've discovered, is that you can't grow this business on your own. No matter how strong or clever you are, or how good you are at delivering your service, or how much exquisite planning you have done – you are always going to need support. This doesn't necessarily mean hiring or building a team; it means all the people in your life, the people you surround yourself with. Everyone in your business and in the relationships you have outside of your business will play a role, and if you're feeling lonely then perhaps you need to take a look at the people you have surrounded yourself with and ask yourself why you feel alone?

As you grow your business and flourish as an entrepreneur, you are going to build relationships with people who will become lifelong friends, partners, companions, confidents and champions. The more you get to know yourself, the clearer you become about the kind of supporters that enhance your life and the closer the bonds you'll form with those people. Some you'll wonder what you ever did without them. Some will give you gifts of wisdom or guidance that will make such a significant impact on you that you will never forget them. And some you know you'll want in your life for good.

The light and shade of this is that as some people become closer, others will drift away. And some relationships *will* actually make you feel like you're doing this on your own. The more difficult truth to accept is that some relationships won't even survive this transition you're making, or at least not in the form that they once were. Some people you will have to actively cut from your business and your life, and I can't sugar-coat this: it will be one of the most difficult and deeply personal decisions you'll come to make.

I once heard a marriage counsellor (married for 22 years) asked: 'How do you stay married to the same person for that length of time?' Her response was – you don't. You don't because as humans we're always growing and evolving, and the person you were 10 years ago will look very different to now. Every now and then you need to check in with one another to see if things are still working for the latest version of both of you.

Now while this all sounds a little contractual for a romantic relationship, it's also pretty rational if you think about it. Why wouldn't you take the time to evaluate your relationship and if it is still working for each of you before, during or after a learning experience? It would certainly save a lot of heartache further down the line if things feel like they're going sideways, and you can jointly assess what's going on (trust me on that one). It could even help repair relationships before they go too far off track. Or in some cases it could make some relationships even stronger. And while this all seems very logical – in reality it's a lot harder to do when you're so emotionally involved.

I believe this is true for your business too. You can't get away from being emotionally involved. It is personal and being able to take a step back and assess your relationships will definitely help with that sense of feeling alone. There is no getting away from how emotionally challenging this is, so everyone needs and deserves a first-class physical, emotional and spiritual team around them. These people are, or will become, your entrepreneuring family… and your friends, supporters, partners, co-founders, customers, mentors, investors and champions for this next amazing phase of your life – choose them wisely.

The important thing is to go in with your eyes open knowing that not all families will be supportive, not all friends will love your baby like you do and not all frogs turn into princes if you kiss them. It's important to realize who you're dealing with and if it brings benefit to both parties to continue your relationship.

People you should seek out, surround yourself with and nurture your relationships with are those who:

- ✓ Make an effort to really get you, the real you and what you're trying to achieve
- ✓ Recognize your ambitions and do what they can to support you
- ✓ Tell the truth and constructively feedback to you with love when they disagree with you
- ✓ Commit to supporting you to achieve that vision
- ✓ Think you're weird but love you anyway
- ✓ Cheer for you and stick with you through rain or shine
- ✓ Grow with you
- ✓ Enable you when you are standing in your own way

✓ Recommend you or say good things about you when you're not there
✓ Emotionally support you when times are tough
✓ Push you to smash through your original beliefs about what you can achieve

Just thinking about the people in my life that fall into that category makes my heart swell a little bit and well, gets me a bit emotional if I'm honest – and they should for you too. If they don't, then they probably fall into the next category. There are people to associate with, tolerate, feel indifferent about, be cautious of or avoid completely. They are people who:

✗ Don't make the effort to really understand what you're about and instead spend their life telling you to get a real job
✗ Have conflicting values or ask you to compromise your values
✗ Seem jealous or critical of your ambitions
✗ Only appear when things are going well and are nowhere to be seen during tough times
✗ Grow apart from you instead of with you
✗ Criticize or force opinions on you when they disagree with you or think you're wrong
✗ Undervalue you and what you offer, or only work with you for their own gain
✗ Never recommend you, talk about you behind your back or only discuss you as part of their own agenda
✗ Flatter you and feed your ego but have no vested interest

Eeuk. No one needs this kind of negativity in their life. Have you got any of these people in your life that you're afraid to distance yourself from because of a misguided fear that you need them or they're adding value? I know I have.

All of these people will help to shape the kind of person and entrepreneur that you want to be. In this chapter, we're going to talk about many of the different kinds of people that you are going to meet or bring along on this adventure with you, as well as how to separate the people that are going to make you feel great from the ones that are going to hold you back or make you feel alone. This is not an exhaustive list! Consider the next sections your guide to choosing your champions well, keeping the good ones close while giving the not so good ones a wide berth.

Family

They say that you can choose your friends, but you can't choose your family. And having family members with you no matter what can be a real bonus if your family falls into the first category of supporters and champions, and not so great if they fall into the second category.

Lucy-Rose and I are very lucky to have mothers who are quite literally our biggest supporters and ambassadors. They encouraged us to be anything we want to be and get quite upset if we're not pushing to be the best at anything we can. Coincidentally, we also both have fathers who are champions *and* entrepreneurs. They bring a totally different outlook on what we're doing that's filled with experience of ups and downs but also admiration and love. We feel really privileged to have had this grounding and it has set us up well for doing what we do.

We know that this is not the case for everyone, and we know what an emotional toll it can take on you when your nearest and dearest just don't get what you're doing.

Gillian Dick – The Go To Agency

My biggest challenge was managing friends and family expectations. I'm an only child and I'm very independent but they would go off and get their monthly pay cheques and that just wasn't for me any more. But I felt as though I had to have this ready-made business for them. I would go to networking events and my dad would ask, 'Have you sold anything?' and I would have to say over and over again: 'It doesn't work like that dad.' I believed that if I went to a networking event and I spoke to two people and they liked me, they might not buy from me, but they might tell someone else, and that is what the game is about.

So, in the first year I went to loads of networking events, but my dad used to just say that it wasn't working for me. It was frustrating, he was being negative without meaning to be, but I found myself telling him less about what I was doing as a result.

I think that's a common reaction to retreat when those around you don't 'get it'. And when family relationships are important and otherwise supportive, then finding strategies to manage this is crucial. We didn't have to do this, but for Gillian her answer was to create her own business family. Through her networking she met many other people who did get her and did get what she was doing. That allowed her to build that vital emotional support network so that dad could just go back to being dad.

On the other hand, if your family have had a similar experience of being in the world of entrepreneuring then it can be a fine line between learning from that experience and feeling like they're constantly involved and not allowing you to forge your own path.

Gary Maitles – The Service Directory

My family are the ones to give me the dose of reality. My brother is an accountant and has his own business and he keeps me grounded when I have an off the wall idea. I think my dad finds it hard to watch me make mistakes and always wants to chip in with advice, whereas I want to make my own mistakes and I want to learn from it.

Them having a business background helps and they get what I'm going through. Likewise, my mum knows what it's like for my wife now because she's been married to an entrepreneur for 50 years. My mum will always joke and say that my dad's business comes first, and my dad always tries to deflect, but he loved his work and he loved developing the business. So, my wife gets the ambition and she gets the workload, but she also pulls me back when it becomes all consuming.

In either of these scenarios, I think it's really important to manage the relationships, keeping in mind that your family will hopefully always come from a position of love and protection. And recognizing they will always do everything they can to prevent you from falling down and hurting yourself.

If you value their relevant experience, then make sure you take it on board objectively and then apply it to your own set of circumstances.

If they become overbearing, then it's perfectly OK to let them know that you are your own person and the way you do this is unique. And that misadventures are OK and perhaps one of the best ways to learn.

Friends

Unlike family, you can choose your friends. I have no doubt that you, like me, have some of the most amazing, loyal, supportive, funny, ambitious and courageous friends that anyone could ask for. That said… friends don't always get it either.

Both Lucy-Rose and I are blessed to have friends who are genuinely interested in what we do and are there every step of the way to support our ambitions. But if you were to ask my friends what it is I actually do, then most of them would shrug! In the past, Lucy-Rose's friends described her as 'the one with the weird jobs' but as they have got older and she has tightened the circle, she now has a group of friends that threw her a surprise party when she became CEO of Entrepreneurial Spark. I'm not trying to be smug here, but I think this is a level of support and friendship that we would all aspire to.

If you were to ask Lucy-Rose about this, it's something that she has never taken for granted and something that she's worked hard to nurture over the years. While I know that even if I've been busy and haven't seen some of my chums in months, I could pick up the phone to them and all would be OK, Lucy-Rose and I joke about her diarizing regular appointments with her friends, and as we mentioned in Chapter 4 on some occasions even scheduling two to three per day to make sure she can fit them all in.

Once again, we realize we're speaking from a position of privilege here, but we do believe that is because we work hard at those relationships, and also because they were strong to begin with. When we spoke to Dan Gregory from Unstoppable Media, he told us this was something he often felt guilty about.

Dan Gregory – Unstoppable Media

I reflected on the quality of my communication with my nearest and dearest with my family and friends or my wife, and I realized that I can be quite short when I am under pressure and I'm working hard on the business and that I am not fully present in that conversation, and that's something that I'm trying to change.

A lot of this is due to overworking so the first thing I need to do is place some significant boundaries around my working time and pledge to finish at a certain time every single day, at a certain time at least 80% of the time to create space for life as well as business. And secondly to actually have quality time with family and friends and schedule out my social life and time to connect with my loved ones.

I think it's all too easy to think that your friends will and should always be there for you, but not everyone is going to be as understanding as you grow and change. We spoke to one entrepreneur who said that just because he doesn't have a nine to five job, his friends say he 'doesn't live in the real world'. We spoke to another entrepreneur who said that her best friend un-friended her on Facebook the day she won her first business award. They simply couldn't cope with her living a new kind of life and making new friends as a result.

Lynn Mann – Supernature Oils

I think in the first few years of the business I felt like I didn't make time for my friends as much as I could, and I felt that I was making new friends in the kind of entrepreneurial world and in business. And then you're just juggling the demands on your time of work and family life. I don't feel as though any of them suffered or I lost any friends as they all seem to have understood. Some relationships have fallen by the wayside, but they probably weren't that strong anyway. I'm much more conscious of who I spend time with now, because I've only got a limited amount of time and I know who I want to spend time with.

Like building your business family, you can include business friends in that too. Lucy-Rose and I didn't know one another before we met at Entrepreneurial Spark. We have a unique relationship that we don't have with any of our other friends because we experience things together that we don't get to experience with anyone else. That doesn't mean we just leave the others behind; it just means that different friends can be there to emotionally support you in different ways and that's OK.

You can choose your friends, and you can choose your business friends; if you are in doubt, refer back to the criteria for people to surround yourself with. Remember that like Lynn, it's OK to let some of those relationships drift too.

Co-founders

If most business ideas are born at the kitchen table or over a few drinks in the pub then it would stand to reason that co-founders mostly begin life as a family member or a friend in some way. But according to Noam Wasserman, Harvard Professor and author of *The Founder's Dilemmas*,[17] one of the most common reasons businesses fail is because of conflict between their founders.

There are loads of ways to fall out with your co-founder and we believe that most of the time it's because business partners are really like life partners. Like choosing a husband or wife, you

---

[17] Noam Wasserman (2013), *The Founder's Dilemmas: Anticipating and Avoiding the Pitfalls That Can Sink a Startup*, Princeton University Press.

wouldn't jump into a marriage without figuring out if you can live with all of their quirks, foibles and skeletons in their closet. And given that you are likely to be spending more time with your co-founder than you would your prospective husband or wife, then your vetting process should be even more stringent than your list of dating do's and don'ts.

Remember the time you first moved in together with someone you were romantically involved with and discovered a whole host of things that drove you crazy about them? The person that once seemed like a great catch looks slightly different in the cold light of unwashed dishes and undergarments on the bathroom floor.

When you co-found a business with someone you experience things together and have conversations that you won't have with anyone else in your life. It's a very special relationship that needs a huge amount of work. Don't be fooled into thinking that just because a person starts as a family member, or a friend, or that you both like your business idea, that you will be suited to be co-founders – choose wisely!

Mike Rucker PhD – Active Wellness

I started a company with my best friend and a friend of ours, and in this type of partnership, I think it's like going into a marriage. However, that isn't necessarily apparent when you start, especially for first-time entrepreneurs. As your start-up evolves, you co-create the company's vision and try to agree upon the roles and boundaries for each founder. But, nine times out of ten, we don't do that as founders because the fear is that we don't know what we don't know. In my case, ultimately, there were things we didn't foresee, but we probably could have if we'd spent the time, in the beginning, to play things forward or done any back casting.

One of the areas where we butted heads as co-founders were around where we wanted to invest our money. Among all employees, we kept base salaries modest, so everyone earned a similar base. As equity partners, however, we could take dividends to augment this as needed. My business partner wanted to spend a significant amount on R&D one year that would really eat into our overall compensation, and we found we were at odds simply because we were at different life stages. I was preparing to eventually get married at the time and was risk averse. In contrast, my co-founder was sharing a small apartment with a roommate and simply had different priorities. Neither of us was wrong; we just had a difference of opinions about risk. We were constructively butting heads at first, but eventually this caused unhealthy friction. As partners, you need to find ways to always ensure that there is an open line of communication – to the extent that you can get in front of some of these issues early on.

Lucy-Rose and I were very lucky in that we worked together before we ran the business together. Lucy-Rose was an original co-founder of Entrepreneurial Spark and I joined a little later. Working together first meant we got to know exactly how each other operated day to day, our strengths and weaknesses and how we made decisions. In that time, we also developed a profound friendship. We learned together from those shared experiences how to get the best from one another. We've supported each other through some of life's hardest challenges, but we're also not afraid to call 'bullsh*t' on each other when it's needed.

That said…. Co-founding is hard!

When Lucy-Rose and I first had the idea of starting Misadventures in Entrepreneuring, we'd had seven years of working together under our belt. A perfect recipe for working together in the future, you would have thought. We know each other's strengths inside out and how to play to them. We also know where each other feels vulnerable and we gently challenge one another to gradually push ourselves in those uncomfortable zones. We believe that we make each other better.

Yet when we stepped out of exit phase and into start-up mode again, things just didn't feel right. And for the self-confessed experts – this is highly uncomfortable and frankly should not be happening!

It came to a head a few months back where we danced around it for about five minutes the way we had been dancing around it for the few months prior to that with a few 'Are you OK?', 'No, are you OK?', 'No, I asked first' type questions before we really got into it. It turns out that being emotionally intelligent and deeply understanding of one another's zones of vulnerability can be both a blessing and a curse.

What we know but hadn't taken into account is that often changes in someone's own personal circumstances can impact that co-founder relationship. We'd been through so much together, but also a massive amount of change in our own lives and we hadn't checked in on that.

We had both noticed changes in each other's behaviour but for reasons of wanting to protect one another, we let it go. Instead, we both got frustrated with the other (in secret we thought) until this spilled over into everyday work where our communication became more perfunctory and business-like in an attempt not to hurt one another, rather than being honest and kind. Ironic.

Instead of leaning in to one another as co-founders, we leaned out as individuals. And when we finally spoke honestly at last there were some tears, some hard questions and some moments of clarity. Ultimately, we both decided we really wanted to continue to work together, but at the same time we both agreed that we didn't want it to continue the way it was.

By the end we wished we'd recorded this conversation because we're pretty sure co-founders must go through this all the time, and instead of addressing the frustration, it's left to fester until the resentment goes so far and feels so personal that you can't come back from it. I've tried to capture the moment in as fresh a way as I can in the hope that it will be helpful to others who might feel this way.

Kerry Harrison opened up to us about the change in dynamic when she and her business partner decided to go into business together after being colleagues in a former business.

Kerry Harrison – Tiny Giant

My co-founder and I used to work together in a former business, so we've known each other for about six years and we're both creative and interested in technology and advertising. He left his job and I was freelancing, and we said: 'Why don't we just do something?' We're really excited about the same things and it's a good time to do it.

It's been interesting as he used to be my boss, but when we became co-founders there were quite a few points where I'd had to say you're not my boss any more; we're actually co-founders. There are a few times when I've had to stand my ground and say 'no' I'm not that person now. We are partners. We have got through that now, but there's still an occasional time. He was always a supportive manager and would pull you under his wing, but now I'm like: 'I'm fine to stand on my own two feet.'

I feel like we're getting through that now though. In terms of the dynamic he's really loud, good at networking and I'm more analytical, detail focused and into planning. We meet in the middle on creativity, passion and driving things forward.

What did we learn from our co-founding experience?

1. Just because something worked before in a previous context, it doesn't mean it can be transplanted into a new situation and fit right away. There needs to be a period of adjustment before anything will function like it did in the past. This requires regular check-ins, refinement and avoiding getting carried away in the momentum.

2. Not speaking up is worse than speaking up and staying silent is never actually silent. You might not say it directly but if you are dissatisfied with someone then you can be sure that it is being communicated in other ways. Always speak up: you might find that the other person isn't aware they are doing something specific and is really grateful that you brought it to their attention. You might also find it's something really simple to resolve.

3. When you co-found with friends, it's easy to let the lines between life and work blur. In fact, it's easy to let a whole load of lines blur and forget that you're building a business together and that needs structure and discipline.

4. It turns out that just talking every day on a video call is not the same as having co-founder check-ins! On reflection, we realized that, yes, we communicate all the time, over-communicate in fact. Video call, email, WhatsApp, social media etc. – it appears on the surface that we are always talking. But have we been talking about the right things? Our next exercise together became a six-month collective vision.

5. If you can't instigate difficult conversations yourself, why not ask someone with less emotional attachment to help?

Getting a mentor or advisor to act as a middle man means they can instigate the questions you might be avoiding and can also play devil's advocate or advise on what makes sense when uncomfortable decisions might need to be made.

If you are in a co-founder relationship, there are always going to be ups and downs in the business and in life, just as there would be in any other personal relationship. And as with any other relationship, we already know that we don't have to be perfect all of the time – it's the open line of communication that is key.

Egos

Let's be frank: sometimes people are just egos on legs. They exist in life and they exist in business too. You'll know who they are as well as we do, and we could probably devote an entire chapter to them alone except I wouldn't want to give them the airtime. The sad fact is that you're going to have to deal with them in some form or another during the course of life and business so you may as well be prepared to recognize them for who they are, rise above it, and most importantly *don't become one*!

The difference between someone genuine and a walking ego is normally characterized by their lack of humility and their need to protect said ego. Some of the most commonly spotted egos include:

- *The Intimidator* – Yes, some people thrive on making others feel small or afraid. If you're feeling particularly vulnerable or out of your comfort zone, then intimidators will inevitably get the best of you. Ignore them if you can. And if you can't then make sure your encounter with an intimidator is immediately followed with either a large gin or a good rant with one of your best supporters.

- *The Bully* – Like intimidators, if bullies don't succeed in cracking you by making you feel small then they'll just bulldoze you to get their own way. Remember that most bullies are bullied themselves; it can definitely help your own bruised ego to empathize with them, then go and get a gin.

- *The Charmer* – Nice to your face, plotting how to get one over on you behind your back. If you can avoid being dazzled by their smile and platitudes to spot their agenda, you'll understand the part you play. Don't be their pawn.

- *The Shark* – Like charmers… but without the charm. They're only out to further their own agenda and they'll be sneaky and backstabbing when they get a chance. These people don't have a conscience and they don't share your values: don't be shark food.

- *The 'W*lly Waggler'* – A senior-level exec in a large corporate once described to us that sometimes people just can't help putting their balls on the table just to make a point. If you think that sounds sexist then I completely agree, and I think this really only applies to anyone who believes that you need to 'have balls' to be in business anyway. We don't. And anyone that throws any of their body parts around to put someone in their place isn't worth associating with. Recognize it for what it is and try not to be intimidated by it.

Gayle and Lucy-Rose, Entrepreneurial Spark – 'That time we were referred to as "ladies in our little fantasy world" during a negotiation'

We can remember one particularly tough business negotiation when we were an all-female team on our side of the table. The negotiations were tough and the conversation was lukewarm; we'd held our own, neither side was conceding very much, and we were almost at stalemate over one particular issue we felt was a deal-breaker. Then, in an attempt to move the conversation along a member of the other team asked us:

'Well, what would you ladies in your little fantasy world suggest we do then?'

We were a little taken aback; though thankfully not shaken enough to put us off our stride. Our suggestion was that the other party go away and try harder on their side and we stood firm that this was a deal-breaker for us. It was definitely a struggle to keep our cool though and if we hadn't done the preparation work going into the negotiation then a comment like that would definitely have succeeded in throwing us off our game.

In the end, there will be egos who will use all of their ego to forward their own agenda, so you need to accept that they exist and decide on your own tactics to deal with them.

The last ego to look out for is your own…

Victoria Green – Victoria Green Ltd

In retrospect, in the early days when the business was growing massively and I was getting loads of awards, I was in danger of becoming a bit of an ego monster. There is sometimes a culture of putting the entrepreneur on a pedestal, which is of course flattering, but it is a testament to my lovely partner that he stuck with me throughout the 'being a d*ck years' when I was consumed by the business and barely thought about anything else, let alone our relationship. A few years later when I went through a sticky patch and some friends and mentors were notable by *their absence, he was there by my side. I could easily have wrecked our relationship by listening to the flattery.*

Mentors

When you're winging it all the time, getting support from people who have been in your shoes can be an excellent idea. One brilliant source of this kind of advice can be to get yourself a mentor. Both Lucy-Rose and I have had mentors for years and each person brings different value to the situations that we're in.

When Lucy-Rose became CEO of Entrepreneurial Spark, she knew it was going to be important to have someone looking out for her in that role, someone she could turn to with the really hard (and sometimes daft) questions that would help to guide her when the buck stopped with her.

I found my first mentor when I began managing a team of people. I had never done it before, and I needed someone who could see qualities in me that I didn't yet know existed and could help me become a leader.

Paul Adams – Goldfish London

I didn't ask for help in the early days. I was self-confident, and I thought I could work through the problems. I ask now especially if people have specialist knowledge. Don't waste your time; find someone who knows what they're talking about and pick their brains. What I have discovered is it's astonishing how free people will be with advice if you ask them. Particularly fellow entrepreneurs as they sympathize with you. I would now not hesitate to ask anyone; I'd connect with them on LinkedIn and message them to say do you mind if I asked for your advice?

Mentors can be invaluable to you as a leader and to your business if, like we've suggested with all relationships, you choose wisely. Take the time to figure out the type of person you want and need for you at the time you need it. What have we learned about working with mentors?

1. All mentors don't have to be old and wise – be honest, when you think of the word 'mentor' you think of someone old don't you? I knew it! Sometimes peer mentors can be just as powerful a source of advice and information than someone who hasn't been in your shoes for a while. Their feelings are not quite as fresh, and they might not be able to see your perspective in the same way as someone who is in the same position or even a few steps ahead.

2. The nature of our Entrepreneurial Spark Hubs and the proximity of entrepreneurs working together meant that natural peer groups formed. When the programme ended for some, they moved into offices together to protect that peer group. Most say that the people they went on the journey with will be friends for life – like Lucy-Rose and I and our shared experiences, sometimes you don't get that with anyone else.

3. Find someone to help you do a job, or someone who just gets you – you can also have different mentors for different stuff. If you don't know anything about sales, then having someone who is a great salesperson mentor you to become a better one can be a really great resource. Likewise, sometimes you just need someone who gets the way you think that can empathize with you and help you to grow into the person you have the potential to become.

4. Lay out the ground rules – if you take the time to think about what you really need then it will help you to brief your mentor and set expectations for your relationship so neither party gets too little nor takes too much. While it might feel like you're taking from a mentor all the time, you'll also find

that they get as much out of it as you do by learning new things from the way you work – like co-mentoring.

5. Don't be a mentor collector – there is such a thing as too much advice! If you have too many people around you giving you their opinions, then it's inevitable that you'll get different perspectives. Too much advice can tie you in knots and leave you overwhelmed. Two great mentors are better than 10 mentors with conflicting viewpoints.

6. You don't have to take their advice – it's great to get a different perspective, but at the end of the day it's your business not theirs, and you have to deal with the consequences of your decisions. It's a fine art to recognize when to take advice and when not to.

7. The rules change when it becomes a commercial relationship – once you've built a great relationship with your mentor, it's tempting to think that they would be a safe hire. This might be something like a non-executive director, or in one of those technical roles that they've been mentoring you in. Just remember that the minute there is money involved then motivators and drivers change, as do the ground rules you set out. Take time to re-evaluate these and don't throw the hiring rules out of the window.

8. It doesn't have to be forever – the best mentors know when their intervention has made a difference and their work is done. If they are a truly great mentor then you will be growing and evolving as a person. You might feel you've outgrown them, and that's OK. The best ones will know this already. Don't be afraid to end the mentor relationship if it feels right. You might need to make room for another mentor to help you get to your next milestone.

The investor

Some investors will be the best things that ever happened to your business, and some won't be. You need to remember that the minute you accept investment in your business, you give away universal control. From taking that loan from your family to get you going, to bringing in an angel or a venture capitalist, investment means that you have to be prepared to share decision making with someone else.

We once heard it described (by an investor) as 'he who has the pesos has the say-so's'. If the idea of this makes your blood run cold, then remember to do your diligence on your investor. Try applying some of the same rules you would use to choose a mentor or a co-founder to figure out if your investor is going to be a good fit for you and your business. This is another example of a relationship that is much like a marriage when you get into it – make sure you're getting into business with someone that respects you and shares your vision and values.

Navigating relationships and bringing people on the adventure with you

The world of entrepreneuring is so full of change that ensuring that all of your human relationships stay intact throughout is going to take a bit of work. As we've heard, some have different expectations, some believe in different things, some are more helpful than you could ever expect, and some will try to force their opinions on you.

These relationships will all be different depending on whether those around you 'get it', have experienced something similar, the strength of the relationship before you started, and who else comes into your life during your adventure.

To avoid misadventuring when choosing who to surround yourself with, try to remember:

- To make time for the really important people in your life and be present.
- To put the effort into taking them on the journey with you – if you want them to be in your life.
- To use your values as guidance in all circumstances.
- To listen to your gut (and then your values) if you believe something is off.
- To have regular, clear and open lines of communication that enable you to be honest and communicate with kindness and empathy.
- To create an entrepreneuring family – the kind you choose.
- It is your business at the end of the day. You can gather advice, but *you* make the final decisions and the buck always stops with you.

Course correction questions

- When was the last time you really checked in with your co-founder? Or partner, or spouse, or anyone else important in your life to see if you're still aligned in what you want from your relationship?
- When was the last time you really played a few scenarios forward to test your alignment?
- Who haven't you brought on the journey with you and does that relationship need attention?
- Who are you spending too much time worrying about?

What do you need to... Stop, Start and Continue doing now?

STOP

- Doing this alone

- Surrounding yourself with egos or people who only have their own agenda at heart

- Getting caught up in the whirlwind of entrepreneuring and forgetting what is important

START

- Surrounding yourself with people who nurture and support you

- Building your business family – this could be different from your real family!

- Checking in with the people you cherish to make sure your relationships are on track – this includes co-founders

- Seeking out mentors and investors who can help with your best interests at heart

CONTINUE

- Bringing people on the adventure with you

- Making time to communicate with all the humans in your life

Bonus exercise: Champions checklist

Think of someone that you are considering working with in your business. It may be a new supplier, customer, mentor or anyone else and use the Champions Checklist to determine if they are someone you should invite into your tribe or not.

(✓) here:

- ☐ Makes an effort to really get you, the real you and what you're trying to achieve
- ☐ Recognizes your ambitions and does what they can to support
- ☐ Tells the truth and constructively feeds back to you with love when they disagree with you
- ☐ Commits to supporting you to achieve that vision
- ☐ Thinks you're weird but loves you anyway
- ☐ Cheers for you and sticks with you through rain or shine
- ☐ Grows with you
- ☐ Enables you when you are standing in your own way
- ☐ Recommends you or says good things about you when you're not there
- ☐ Emotionally supports you when times are tough

☐ Pushes you to smash through your original beliefs about what you can achieve

(✖) here:

☐ Doesn't make the effort to really understand what you're about and instead spends their life telling you to get a real job
☐ Has conflicting values or asks you to compromise your values
☐ Seems jealous or critical of your ambitions
☐ Only appears when things are going well and is nowhere to be seen during tough times
☐ Grows apart from you instead of with you
☐ Criticizes or forces opinions on you when they disagree with you or think you're wrong
☐ Undervalues you and what you offer, or only works with you for their own gain
☐ Never recommends you, talks about you behind your back or only discusses you as part of their own agenda
☐ Flatters you and feeds your ego but has no vested interest

7

Misadventures in...

GETTING STUCK

**(Because no great story ever ended with
'...and that was exactly what I expected to happen')**

When I joined Entrepreneurial Spark back in 2012, original co-founder Jim Duffy asked me a question during my interview. He asked: 'Is the global recession an obstacle or an opportunity for entrepreneurs?'

I was a little taken aback at the time as it wasn't the kind of question that I had been expecting during the interview and as I ran through the question in my mind, I found myself in an internal debate. My natural stance at that point was to go for obstacle. The economy was in chaos, nothing was certain, we were operating in a time of austerity, our currency had devalued, people were losing their jobs – surely this could not be a good thing?

Then a small light bulb went on. Actually... maybe this is a good time for entrepreneurs, maybe the best even? When nothing can be relied upon this creates opportunity? The opportunity to do things differently, to shake things up, to be innovative, to show customers, business and governments that there can be new ways of doing things?

Wait a minute, the debate went on… what if I had a business at the time that the recession hit? Would that not send my business into turmoil? Supplier prices would rise; I may have to lay people off. The very entrepreneurs who seek opportunity may come in and steal some of my market share? How would I cope? This would be terrifying and the thought of having to deal with that on a daily basis must be so stressful! This feels like a real obstacle.

Isn't this a good thing? Said my devil's advocate. It prevents you from becoming stagnant, forces you to reinvent what you are doing regularly, stay ahead of the competition, keep an eye on the macro environment and stops you from resting on your laurels. It prevents you from becoming resilient and adaptable to change and teaches you new ways to overcome obstacles.

I realize I could go on all day arguing both sides of the debate and, in reality, most of this internal dialogue was actually external. I could see Jim's eyes beginning to roll a little, pleading me to come to a conclusion eventually.

Needless to say, I never did come to a conclusion, because I didn't realize what I was debating at the time. But I definitely believe now that the answer is not in whether or not this is an obstacle or an opportunity – the answer of course lies in what you perceive it to be, and how you respond or adapt accordingly that makes it so.

I also believe this about any situation where we come across obstacles in our path. Do you choose to let the obstacle stand in your way, or do you choose to figure out how to move it, climb it or dance around it jubilantly? There's a saying that goes: 'Dear Pessimist and Realist – while you were busy arguing about the glass of water – I drank it. Sincerely, The Optimist.' It is the way that we choose to respond and our subsequent action that can cause us to have plenty of moments of misadventure.

There are positives to obstacles, changeable circumstances and unknown outcomes. They create opportunity to do things in new and different ways; they teach us to become problem solvers and figure out new solutions. In entrepreneuring exponential, technological change now means that markets once dominated by Fortune 500 companies are rapidly being replaced by smaller and more agile businesses (like us) who are able to be more responsive to market changes (in theory); opportunity is everywhere.

And if you aren't frightened off by the idea of figuring out how to do things differently, then this changeable landscape could be the perfect space for entrepreneurs like you to play. This chapter is about recognizing that change is now our new norm, and that we don't always respond the way we think we will when change actually happens. It's easy to find yourself in an unhelpful pattern of thinking and to get yourself stuck without realizing. This chapter is about building your awareness of the inevitability of change and about learning to thrive in the unknown.

The inevitability of the unknown, change and getting stuck

People change and societal norms never stop evolving, from environmental sustainability, veganism and electric cars to the latest fashion or beauty trends. As entrepreneurs we would be very remiss if we are not literally waiting for our customers, markets and the world to shift in front of our very eyes. If you don't believe me then believe this – recently, my partner's nine-year-old son asked me what a butcher was...

As humans, we cope pretty well with change as a whole – when it is our choice *and* when it happens at a pace that doesn't scare us. Giant societal shifts don't happen overnight and we have time to become accustomed to them. We can cope with the kind of change that we have a long run up to prepare for.

Yet it's the everyday obstacles, unexpected events and unplanned changes that we didn't predict, or that fly out of left field that tend to leave us scratching our heads a bit. And the funny thing about us entrepreneurs is that despite already knowing that by nature what we're doing is taking a step into the unknown, that there is a high probability of coming across things we didn't anticipate every day, we can't help but seem somewhat surprised when it actually happens.

That's the bit that makes this whole entrepreneuring business hard and the part that no one tells you from the outset. This is what entrepreneuring is all about. It's not about having the best product or raising investment or hiring a great team – it is all of that too. But it's mostly about becoming an absolute specialist in adapting your plans and not letting obstacles set you back or prevent you from getting stuck. This is a test of your patience, your resilience and your ability to keep making progress despite these changes and uncertainty.

Mandy Bailey – Plant 'n' Grow

Prepare yourself personally, make sure you're resilient enough for the journey and if you think you're not, go away and work at it, definitely work at it. Because in times of crisis and on the bad days everyone will look at you, they will take their lead from you and you need to stay strong for that. It takes a bit of work to become resilient and I think we forget that; it gets lost in the excitement of 'let's get going, I've got this fantastic idea' and even if you tick all the boxes you're sometimes not ready until you hit the crisis. The important thing is making sure you are ready for the journey you are about to go on.

It goes a bit like this:

You begin by taking all the knowledge, experience and planning and you get started. It's a risk, but a calculated one. You feel like you know what you're doing, you're in your comfort zone, decisions are going well, and outcomes are in line with your expectation. It feels like you are running downhill and the wind is at your back.

And then, just when you think you've got things figured out, you don't feel like you're winging it any more – something comes along and throws a spanner in the works. An unexpected turn of events that means you have to rethink what you're doing.

Your perception of the severity of the event will influence your reaction. Not everyone gets stuck here and it's entirely possible to be unphased by things that others might see as a total disaster. Do you react like a gliding swan frantically pedalling underneath the surface as you recalibrate, or do you go into full toddler meltdown mode and end up stuck spinning your wheels in mud?

How you cope will depend on how hardy you are feeling that day or that hour. If this is the first or the fifteenth time something hasn't gone to plan and it's getting a bit wearing. It will depend on your inbuilt resilience and your ability to stop yourself from spiralling, and it will depend on your ability to reimagine your situation in alternative ways.

Here are a couple of scenarios from our own playbook to show you the process in action.

Unexpected scenario 1

Three people resign from your business in the space of two weeks, each giving four weeks' notice, but your recruitment process takes three months to complete. Your funder is questioning your company culture and in your head you're likening your business to 'rats from a sinking ship'.

Response option 1: Stuck

You are unable to see the funny side. You listen to your funders, question your company culture and fall into a downward spiral of believing that you are to blame, and this could crush you. You can't hit your funders' KPIs and your funding is at risk. You are depressed and struggle to see a way forward.

Response option 2: Reimagined

You lie on the floor (behind the door), call your business partner, have a laugh at how hugely perplexing and unfortunate this is, one cries, the other stays logical and vice versa until you pull yourselves together and you make a plan. You use this as an opportunity to revisit the way you deliver your business and come up with a new and innovative model. Your business is more flexible and adaptable as a result.

Response option 3, 4, 5...: Reimagined in any way your mindset can

This is a true story. Our true story.

Unexpected scenario 2

You sign a brand new distributor who orders 1,500 boxes of your all-natural dog biscuits for their first listing in three weeks' time. The next day your manufacturer tells you that they can no longer produce your product and cannot fulfil the order. In fact, not only can they not fulfil the largest order in the history of your business; they can't fulfil any order. They are dumping you as a client – and did I mention it was four days before Christmas?

Response option 1: Stuck

You are unable to see the bright side. You believe that this is a test you will not pass. You are unable to fulfil the orders; you believe that your distributor will delist you as a result. This could be the end of your business. You tell no one; you succumb to your worst fears.

Response option 2: Reimagined

You go to your local accelerator hub and tell your fellow entrepreneurs what has happened. You listen to 10 minutes of 'are you kidding' and 'you can't be serious' – you wish you were. Everyone offers suggestions, every one of which you could reject. But you don't, because you've done a bit of laughing and a bit of crying, as has everyone else around you. And when all of the tears have dried up you now have a working plan that involves hiring a catering kitchen where 23 entrepreneurs spend the 27 December making 1,500 boxes of all-natural dog biscuits. Everyone is laughing. Order fulfilled; business saved.

Response option 3, 4, 5...: Reimagined in any way your mindset can

This is a true story (someone else's).

How do you respond?

When it comes to responding to an unexpected event, the level that this affects you and your ability to see your options will determine how quickly and easily you can recover or bounce back and get going again.

See if you recognize any of these:

a) Shocked and surprised

You're dazed and confused like someone has played a practical joke on you and candid camera is going to appear at any moment. Commonly recognized from phrases like:

> *'You are kidding?'*
> *'You're having a laugh?'*
> *'You can't be serious?'*
> *'Are you joking?'*

When you are shocked and surprised, this is usually not enough to get you stuck. You didn't know something was possible but now you do. You should fairly easily be able to have a cup of tea, chalk it up to experience, alter your plans a little to overcome a slight hurdle and keep going.

You may be the type of person that when a shock happens, you're better to be in action than sitting still. If you are, then use this. Make a quick response plan and keep moving.

And don't forget, seeing the funny side is never a bad option. I'm not saying that every time something difficult happens you should laugh it off and carry on but I do believe there is definite merit in trying to see the funny side of a misadventure before the self-pity takes hold and you begin to wallow in it.

b) Panic

What if…

>   …*no one comes?*
>   …*my customers hate me?*
>   …*no one buys anything?*
>   …*the staff all leave?*
>   …*everyone thinks I'm stupid?*

Similar to shock, panic mode has the ability to paralyse. Often this is just an adrenaline spike or the fight or flight part of your brain reacting to what has just happened.

I was once eating lunch with Lucy-Rose in the canteen of our building when she received a text message that immediately put her into panic mode. She promptly got up from her chair and ran out of the room. I then saw her tear across the car park and sit in the passenger seat of her car. This is a time to find a safe space, take a minute until the flight reaction calms itself.

c) Denial

Where shock turns to disbelief and something is genuinely unbelievable or unthinkable then it can take a bit longer to get going. Characterized by mild rumination and oscillating between a state of shock and disbelief. You're telling yourself (and others):

>   *'Surely not?'*
>   *'Huh?'*
>   *'Wow?'*
>   *'That can't be right'*
>   *'I never expected that'*
>   *'Is this really happening?'*

Denial is not as easy to overcome as surprise or temporary panic. You might need to take longer to get moving again as you come to terms with something that you can't quite believe really happened or feels out of your control. This is a job for a doughnut, or a gin. Or a lie down on the floor behind the office door with the blinds pulled down, or inside a cupboard. Something to feel like it might minimize the impact of the shock, or if you hide or lie down it might go away somehow.

This has the potential to turn into a temporary stuck situation if you find it difficult to come to terms with the new reality and your part in it.

d) Frustration and resistance

You've come to terms with the facts, and now you're annoyed and frustrated. My favourite thing to do at this point is find someone else to blame. Or a good run in self-flagellation is also a popular internal monologue. It sounds a bit like:

> 'I knew something like this was going to happen, I'm so angry at myself for not spotting it before now.'

> 'How could I let this happen? I'm so stupid.'

> 'How on earth could x or y person allow this to happen? Surely they must have seen this coming!'

Two popular alternative hallmark responses are:

1. Allow someone else to offer you 100 new ways to overcome what has happened and then flatly reject each and every one in turn in favour of clinging to your original plan and pretending like nothing has happened.

2. Pretend like this is the worst thing that has ever happened, and the world is going to end imminently if it doesn't go back to the way you originally planned.

This has the potential to turn into a real stuck situation. When you start to dish out blame then you are avoiding taking responsibility. Did you create this situation? Or have you become a victim of it? The only way back from this kind of response is to recognize that these thoughts aren't going to get you anywhere. Another easy one to say but harder to do problem. Fortunately, you are only stuck because you can't see beyond the limits of your thinking, conditioning even. You have the power to turn this around, but it might involve a bit of introspection and taking a look at your part in what happened, or your part in how you've responded.

Have a good cry or a scream. Who doesn't love a good cry; go on, let it all out. Then take ownership of what happens next – that bit is up to you. What has to change? What do you need to learn? What do you need to unlearn to start to get going again?

You are well and truly stuck and you're not getting out of this one without some serious perspective adjustments.

With every level of stuckness so far you are learning and storing information in the memory banks that will help you to reimagine your way back to moving again the next time something like this happens, and you're building resilience. The wind doesn't really feel at your back any more and it certainly feels like more of an uphill exercise, but you're still going and you're a better version of your entrepreneurial self for it.

Lauren Valler – Habakuk Recruitment

My mind is frazzled; I feel like the business has so much potential and I have the potential to drive it forward, but I've had a few hits along the way that have made me question everything. I know that's a deep statement to make but it's around the quality of my life and being strong. That's where I am at this moment.

Yes, there's been a few tears, a lot of tears, let's be real. And fear of the unknown and what does my future look like? It's really difficult to plan something you don't have full confidence in. For once in my life, I am usually an ambitious young woman, but right now I don't feel like that. I've been going around and round... my poor notebook!

Back in Chapter 1 we discussed that the premise of this entire book was built around the fact that it doesn't matter where you are now; you have to embrace the fact that you are (almost) always the problem and the solution to becoming great.

When you're stuck, the only way to get unstuck is to realize that it's your response that's keeping you stuck. Your attitude towards your predicament is the one keeping you there. I realize that if you are stuck right now then this isn't going to be something that you're going to want to hear and the urge to throw this book across the room (or drop it in the bin) is going to be a strong one. You might be thinking:

'How could you possibly know what I'm going through right now?'

'Try being in my shoes and you'll see it's not as easy as that.'

'How can the fact we're running out of cash possibly be resolved by changing my attitude?'

'I am completely underwater and simply don't have enough hours in the day to do what needs to be done; why are you telling me that I am the problem to being stuck?'

And you're going to hate me even more when I promise you it's the truth. You might not be able to see it now, and you might have to go through your own process to get to the place of being able to recognize it. But one day soon you will, and then you'll make a mental note of this moment for the next time.

When you're ready, let's take a breath and think about a different time when you were stuck. This is going to be a writing or drawing bit just because if you commit it to paper, you're much more likely to act on it. Scary I know.

We've provided some space below, but you can also use a different piece of paper or your misadventures journal if, like me, you're scared to mess up the pages of your book.

OK, here we go.

Firstly, describe the situation in as much detail as you can. Only focus on the facts at the moment; no feelings just yet.

_____

_____

_____

_____

_____

_____

_____

_____

Now describe how you were feeling about it. Make sure you include anyone or anything you felt was to blame.

_____

_____

_____

_____

_____

_____

_____

_____

_____

Also describe what you were doing while you were feeling that way.

_____

_____

_____

_____

_____

_____

_____

_____

_____

Now, describe when you began to feel better and what you were doing at the time.

_____

_____

_____

_____

_____

_____

_____

_____

_____

Lastly, describe what happened next and how the situation was resolved.

_____

_____

_____

_____

_____

_____

_____

_____

_____

Looking back on that scenario, what could you learn from being stuck and from becoming unstuck again? What was it about the event that was so unexpected that it rendered you in some form of stuck response?

Thinking about the next time you find yourself stuck, what can you learn from this time that will help you to recognize when you are stuck the next time? What can you do to make the process of getting to a place of reimagination and overcoming an obstacle quicker the next time?

Here's another true story.

A number of years ago, Lucy-Rose and I had just taken the reins of Entrepreneurial Spark together. I had moved into the role of COO and director of the company and she was a director and CEO. We were learning this new dynamic as two female leaders and how to work best with people external to the business who had previously had experience of working with Lucy-Rose's predecessor Jim Duffy alongside Lucy-Rose.

As duos we were very different, and Lucy-Rose was keen to demonstrate her style of leadership rather than being seen as Jim's replacement. However, our challenges began when some of our key relationships began to change and people who we had been used to dealing with in a different capacity were unsure of how best to work with us in our new positions. While some welcomed our approach with open arms, some were hesitant, and some were not comfortable at all.

After a short while, it began to be a problem for us as meetings were strained, some key relationships had become rocky and it was distracting us from achieving what we wanted to achieve.

We'd become defensive and we were coming away from meetings and phone calls like they were a waste of time. We began to become upset with some of those we were working with, feeling as though they were upset at the change and didn't want to work with us as individuals. We believed that they were to blame for the breakdown in relations; we believed that they were treating us with hostility and resentment, choosing unhelpful language and tactics. At this point we began fighting fire with fire.

We weren't enjoying our roles or our day to day and it felt like a slog. At the same time we were also working on developing ourselves as leaders. We were figuring out what kind of leaders we were, what our superpowers were, how we could communicate most effectively with our teams, what the vision for the business was and how we would execute on that.

Lucy-Rose suggested we meet a coach to help us develop our self-awareness and achieve some of our individual and collective goals. It wasn't until we began working with that coach that we realized that how we were perceived externally played a huge part in what we were trying to achieve. When we took ourselves out of the frustrating scenario, we were suddenly able to see that we had become hostile and resentful and our language and the way we were responding was equally unhelpful. We were stuck in a cycle of behaviour that went back and forward between us and other people and was becoming increasingly unproductive.

With the help of our coach we were able to take a step back and understand that we played just as big a part in breaking this cycle as everyone else involved, and a shift in our attitude could have a big difference on the attitudes of others. He reminded us that the only people we could control were ourselves, but even then, we'd lost control of our own emotions and behaviours. We were going into meetings expecting the outcome to be negative and, well, you can guess what the outcome was.

Our coach challenged us to work on our mindset before we went to meetings, wrote emails or talked on the phone. We practised setting our RAS[18] (Reticular Activating System), which he explained was like a giant net that caught and filtered all the thoughts and words you say to yourself every day. Your RAS captures the most common ones and then assumes you want more of them, so it focuses your mind in that direction, like when you decide that you're going to buy a red car and then suddenly all you seem to see on the road are red cars.

The trouble is that your RAS can't distinguish between helpful or hindering thoughts, so we had to train ourselves to set ourselves up for a positive outcome rather than the negativity that we had been expecting before.

He challenged us to not react to triggers and slip back into defensive behaviours, only to focus on what we were trying to achieve. And he taught us to tune in to the emotions and expectations of others involved. If they were already expecting a battle and that's what they received, then we'd be back to square one. He coached us to take ownership of our side of the relationship and be accountable for our behaviour, rather than trying to make excuses or lay blame. I'm pleased to say that it really worked and had a huge impact on the way we interacted from that point on.

---

[18] Myia Cleggett (2015), 'Change your life with the Reticular Activating System', *Mind Motivation Coaching*. Available from: www.mindmotivationcoaching.com/blog/change-your-life-with-the-reticular-activating-system [accessed March 2020].

It was also a series of incredible life lessons. It taught us to prepare for challenging events functionally but also emotionally. It taught us to use our emotional intelligence that we'd somehow misplaced in favour of our egos and tune in to the people we were interacting with as humans, not adversaries.

Not only did this get us unstuck on that occasion, but many more since. These are life lessons we will never forget, and I have no doubt we became better entrepreneurs as a result.

On this occasion, it took a coach to hold a mirror up to our behaviour to get us unstuck. We were just fortunate enough to already be working with that coach in other areas so he was able to help us help ourselves before the situation got out of control. This was something we trained our team to do every day with and for entrepreneurs, but without our own coach we weren't able to see the wood for the trees.

Course correction questions

- The last time you got stuck, how did you respond?
- What was it about the event that was so unexpected that it rendered you stuck?
- How long did it take to get unstuck and move forward, and what did you learn from that?
- How will you recognize when you are stuck the next time? And who could you ask to help you with it?

What do you need to... Stop, Start and Continue doing now?

STOP

- Fretting that things will change: it is inevitable. This is your world now

- Allowing yourself to become unnecessarily stuck by recognizing when you are self-sabotaging

- Blaming others for being stuck and not recognizing your part in it

START

- Understanding how you respond to change in different situations by reflecting on situations where you were stuck and learning from them

- Recognizing where you are keeping yourself stuck by picking up on signals from past situations

- Unsticking yourself faster and more effectively by using your learning when you first recognize you're starting to feel like you are not responding well

---

   ◉   Setting your RAS for success

CONTINUE

   ◉   Moving to new levels of self-awareness

   ◉   Progressing at pace and smashing obstacles in your way

---

Bonus exercise: Thinking errors

Most of the time we become stuck, it's because we're having a 'Thinking Error'. David D Burns, MD writes about different types of thinking errors in his book *Feeling Good: The New Mood Therapy*.[19]

They include:

All or Nothing Thinking	Sometimes known as black or white thinking, this is where you can only see one way or the other, rather than the variations in between. E.g. It's either a success or it's a failure.
Over Generalizing	Taking the outcome of a single event and then applying it to every situation without considering the individual circumstances. E.g. When a customer says no and you believe all customers will do the same.
Filtering Out the Positive	Being so focused on a single negative that you filter out all of the positives. E.g. You have one bad day and suddenly your whole week is a disaster.

---

[19] David D Burns, MD (2012), *Feeling Good: The New Mood Therapy*, Harper. Reprint Edition.

Mind Reading	Making assumptions about what other people are thinking based on your own opinions and without evidence. My error of choice – see below.
Catastrophizing	A slippery slope of negative thoughts that quickly turn an unfavourable situation into the end of the world. E.g. That one didn't work and suddenly everything is ruined!
Emotional Reasoning	When we feel something and then we believe it to be true, just because we feel that way. E.g. I feel fat therefore I must be fat.
Labelling	Putting a mental label on a person or an event and then categorizing it in that way consistently. E.g. That sales call scared me so now all sales calls are scary.
Fortune Telling	Predicting what is going to happen in the future based on your beliefs rather than facts and creating self-fulfilling prophecies. E.g. This sales call isn't going to go well, and then it doesn't because of your attitude.
Personalization	A little like mind reading, you assume that other people behave in certain ways because of you. E.g. That customer didn't call back because they didn't like me.
Unreal Ideal	Comparing yourself or your successes against someone else when your individual circumstances are completely different. E.g. They've got themselves together; I should have to do so too.

One thinking error I am incredibly prone to is *Mind Reading*. When you are having a mind reading thinking error all you can focus on is what you assume another person might be thinking about a given situation... based on no evidence whatsoever! My inner narrative sounds a bit like:

'Wow, they must think I'm an idiot.'

'Gosh, they must think I don't know what I'm doing.'

And many other variations. These have the power to paralyse you if you begin to believe in your assumptions. Your bonus exercise for this chapter is to read through all of the Thinking Errors slowly and then:

1. Ask yourself which one most resonates with me?
2. Think of a time when you last fell into this thinking error. What situation did it create?
3. How could you have dealt with the situation differently by thinking differently?

Now actively watch for your thinking errors in everyday life and think about how you can address them and begin to change them.

8

Misadventures in...

OVERCOMING OBSTACLES

Self-awareness is going to be your greatest superpower when it comes to tuning in to your response mechanisms. Adapting your behaviour or learning to turn what seems like a negative situation on the surface into a positive outcome is a gifted capability. What if I could tell you that I could make it even easier for you? Interested?

How to get mentally stronger, more resilient and get over obstacles consistently

We know that the only constant in your world as an entrepreneur is change. Great entrepreneurs are true masters of overcoming challenges by building their mental strength and flexibility and you can only achieve that if you're willing to put the work in to *yourself*. But it's hard to do that when your back is against the wall.

This chapter is going to focus on a kind of mental training that you can do to build that capability when the pressure is off... So that when the pressure is on, you're better and more prepared than you've ever been.

Here are three kinds of mental training you can do:

1. Take time to learn from your misadventures.
2. Practise pushing past your boundaries.
3. Learn to reimagine daily.

Take time to learn from your misadventures

The worst-kept secret in learning how to respond differently in a situation is (drum roll)… to reflect on what happened and what you can learn from it. Seriously, it's that simple.

Yes, I know you're thinking, 'Why do I need a book to tell me the blooming obvious?' Here's what I'm thinking. When we started our own business, we struggled to reflect and learn from it ourselves. If you don't take the time to do this, and I mean actually do this and not just give it lip service, you're just going to find yourself right back in that same situation.

So, regardless of how you react, when things don't go to plan it can feel a bit crap. It's OK and perfectly natural to spend time licking your wounds and feeling a little sorry for yourself. When you are ready the next important step to build your mental strength is to reflect on what happened and what you can learn from it. Trust me.

Mike Rucker PhD – Active Wellness

My first endeavour into entrepreneurship was successful and I had a good exit, but it left me very cocky. Technically I was undefeated, so I went into my next endeavour thinking I couldn't fail. I thought if I put everything I have into the next project I can't go wrong! The second company was building a Mexican cantina on the beach in the Los Angeles area. I planned a six-month launch, I had just finished my MBA, I had the right mentors, and I was ready to go. Time to hustle!

I started to build out the location; I jumped into signing the lease. Getting started wasn't that hard the last time, so I didn't want to overthink anything, I didn't want to overspend on legal counsel. Ultimately though, the build was slower than I hoped. Then during the build, I found out the plumbing was rusted and the six-month commercial lease warranties initially protecting me had expired. I found myself on the hook for these unforeseen repairs... about $90k, and I was only projecting to make that much profit in the first three years. It was a terrible time; it knocked me on my arse. I had to re-evaluate everything from there on in.

You have to give yourself time to grieve when things go wrong. Know what your threshold is, so it is not a moving target that runs you into the ground. As entrepreneurs, when we begin this journey and lack experience in entrepreneurship, we can make poor decisions because failure is painful, and we want to avoid pain. When you are able to predetermine and commit to a threshold it can make painful decisions easier. For example, at year one, here are my expectations... then check in with yourself. If they don't match, will you go on? It would be best if you also separate your business from who you are as a person. The hero's journey doesn't always end in success. Just because your business failed doesn't make you the 'person' a failure.

The reason that I know I have to tell you to reflect and the reason I know that you're probably not doing it, or enough of it, is because it's actually quite a hard thing to do. Proper reflection time requires us to do two things that don't come naturally to us entrepreneurs who are always seeking forward motion. They are:

1. Sit still.
2. Give conscious consideration to the past.

I don't know about you, but I am a classic over-thinker. I am the epitome of the meme:

> *My mind is like an internet browser. 19 tabs open, 3 of them are frozen and I have no idea where the music is coming from.*

The thought of sitting still and giving conscious consideration to the way that I behaved in any given scenario is terrifying. To my mind I have already over-thought it, over-analysed it and over-catastrophized it. Giving it any more thought is likely to burn a hole in the side of my head. Or so my overthinking brain is telling me.

What I have now learned from years of coaching, enablement, counselling and hanging about with Lucy-Rose is that by not sitting still, taking a breath, doing the deep reflective work and understanding how my responses affected the outcome of any given situation, I am preventing myself from tapping in to a goldmine of insight that lives right there in my brain. And this will actually help me to make better decisions, not hold me up.

This applies to situations where I responded well as much as it does to situations where I responded not so well. And never was it more prevalent than when I was managing a team. I recognize that as a manager my attitude towards setting high standards for myself and others (driven by my values) made me quite a demanding person to work for. Always striving to do more, always looking to better our approach and always driving continuous improvement. There was always a danger that in among that desire to be better, I inadvertently forgot that my team were human beings!

On one occasion after the team delivered a really successful event, I gathered them together for a debrief the next morning. After covering the niceties and the congratulations, I immediately (and ironically) went straight into what we could learn from the event and what would make the next event even better. After a moment, the team politely asked if it was OK that they just enjoy the success of the event and work on the improvements the next day. I was taken aback. It wasn't that I hadn't recognized their achievements, but I had failed to recognize that they deserved the time to savour and learn from them.

After that I worked exceptionally hard on making sure that I took a moment and gave conscious consideration to tune in to my team, their feelings and their efforts. I know from personality profiling that my decision making is driven by logical fact and process, not feelings and emotions, so I had to work extra hard to develop that element of my management style, sometimes writing at the top of my to-do list every day 'check in with team before anything else'.

It paid dividends. My team felt valued and heard and as a result were happier and more productive in their roles. And as research cited[20] in a *Harvard Business Review* (HBR) article in 2017[21] shows, 'employees who spent 15 minutes at the end of the day reflecting about lessons learned performed 23% better after 10 days than those who did not reflect'.

Taking time to reflect on your misadventures will only build your capacity to overcome obstacles more effectively in the

---

[20] Giada Di Stefano, Francesca Gino, Gary Pisano and Bradley R. Staats (14 June 2016), 'Making experience count: The role of reflection in individual learning', Harvard Business School NOM Unit Working Paper No. 14-093. Available from: https://ssrn.com/abstract=2414478 or http://dx.doi.org/10.2139/ssrn.2414478 [accessed February 2020].
[21] Jennifer Porter (21 March 2017), 'Why you should make time for self-reflection (even if you hate doing it)', *Harvard Business Review*. Available from: https://hbr.org/2017/03/why-you-should-make-time-for-self-reflection-even-if-you-hate-doing-it [accessed March 2020].

future. Recognizing where you can learn to respond more helpfully in the future will stand you in good stead the next time you find yourself out of your comfort zone.

The same HBR article finishes by quoting Peter Drucker:

> *Follow effective action with quiet reflection. From the quiet reflection, will come even more effective action.*

Practise pushing past your boundaries

Resilience and mental strength aren't things that are already inbuilt in us: we weren't born with a resilience bone that you do or don't have. It's more like a muscle that grows over time, which is exercised in situations that require it. The more times you encounter setbacks and overcome challenges, the more the muscle will grow.

Scott Newby – Newby Core Consulting

> *You learn so much and it's a steep learning curve and there are times when I've thought I've made a mistake. It's not for the faint-hearted.*
>
> *There's lots of intangibles to learn, ask for advice, meet new people and take a lot from clients I work with. I'm always learning 24/7; I'm a lot more open and understanding after sharing my story. There are times where you have to delve deep in terms of resilience and I'm stronger for it. Practically I'm better at carving out time in the day to read up on new things and stick to that rather than all the time.*
>
> *Am I good enough, have I got the capability? You question this. I've been good at work and sport, but then you start to have self-doubt, maybe I'm not capable and have to tell*

people I only did it for a month? But I think it's OK to be vulnerable and not know everything.

You can also proactively exercise your resilience muscle by purposefully challenging yourself. It's this kind of soul-searching and asking yourself tough questions that has been an integral part of this book. This will help you to continue to grow and ensure you never rest on your laurels or consider yourself the finished article.

This is the sort of thing you can do when you are feeling mentally strong, not when you are in the thick of it or it will only serve to make you feel more vulnerable. So, the next time you feel like things have been going well for you for a while, why not nudge yourself in the direction of a new challenge? If you can get over the discomforting and sometimes painful nature of growth, it can be hugely rewarding as you understand more and more about your untapped potential and how capable you actually are.

I like to think about it a bit like DOMS.

DOMS

If you are unfamiliar with DOMS, this stands for Delayed Onset Muscle Soreness, which is normally associated with a punishing physical workout and can last for one to three days afterwards. You will probably know the pain of trying to get up out of bed after overdoing it on the abs or walking upstairs after a run (or downstairs for that matter).

What's happening here is a sign that you've worked hard: you've pushed yourself out of your comfort zone. You've caused tiny micro-tears in your muscles and your body is in recovery mode, patching you up and getting you ready for the next workout.

After a few days the pain has subsided: in its place you have grown new, better and stronger muscle tissue.

It's only through experiencing that regularly during physical workouts that I realized you actually go through a similar process when you put the hardest working muscle in your body – your brain – through the wringer too.

Take the state of resistance as an example. The world around you has changed and your brain is trying to cope with the new reality but it's wrestling with it. It's in a tug of war between hankering for what was and searching for what could be. It's tired from you beating yourself up and exhausted from warding off impending doom. In order to clamber out of this situation you need to dig deep into the resilience stores. You might need to seek help to understand how you are limiting yourself, causing yourself to be stuck. You need to break the autopilot that you have been cruising along with to find a new perspective.

DOMS is proof that you've worked hard to push past your previous limitations. It's a frighteningly unknown but exhilarating place and once you have experienced it, it becomes somewhat addictive to finally know that you are capable of far more than you originally considered.

Your progress might start to look a bit like this…

This comes down to carving out time and energy to do the mental workouts. A friend suggested to me recently to try to replace one of my physical workouts a week with a self-development session. She encouraged me to book it in with a start and end time like I would do with a spin class. I have to admit, I felt just as refreshed and almost as self-righteous as if I'd been in the gym!

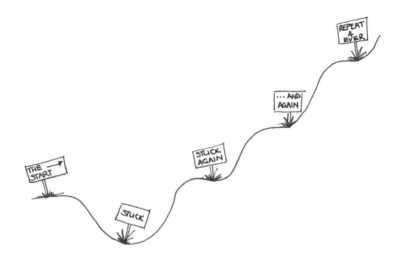

Paul Thomas – Paul Thomas Digital

My kids are enjoying an Inset day today – a day for their teachers to learn, plan and get set for the new year, booked into the calendar as protected time each term. Having just read a great post on underinvesting in personal development, I've decided to add 'Inset days' to my working calendar, once every other month (or monthly?!), to help carve out time to work on myself, rather than directly on my business.

A final word of caution here is that there is a difference between challenging yourself when you are mentally strong and pushing yourself too far when you are not ready. Like any physical sport, if you push yourself too far, too fast, then you are likely to cause yourself an injury. Pushing your mental boundaries comes with the same common-sense limitation. Challenge yourself in a healthy way and beware of burnout.

Learn to reimagine daily

Breaking your own autopilot, pushing past the limitations of your current thinking and being able to take a fresh perspective on a challenge or obstacle is another learned behaviour that can be developed by exercising it.

It's a form of creativity that can be used in complex problem-solving situations to come up with an endless stream of alternative options to the one that is in front of you. If you've never challenged yourself to come up with more than 10 uses for a pencil that don't include writing, sketching and drawing, then start practising.

For some people, spending time doing this is going to feel like an unnecessary luxury. Just another thing that you feel as though you are too busy to do. For others, it might be something you practise regularly. If, like Lucy-Rose and I, you have anxiety then you'll be in the category of people who have no option but to reimagine 100 different scenarios at any moment, which ironically may make you absolutely excellent at handling unexpected events because you've already planned for most of them in your head.

One of the exercises you can use to practise and hone your reimagination muscle is to reimagine the way you currently do business. This is really simple to do and it can help you to generate ideas to take your business in a new direction. Or it could prove to be a lifeline if, for any reason, you had to stop doing business the way you are doing it now.

The idea is that you take your business and then reimagine the way you deliver it – as if it were a completely different business. Let's try:

Q. Reimagine your business as if you were to give away a basic product or service for free and then charge for a premium-level product or service. Like LinkedIn, or most apps. What would it look like?

A. If we were to imagine this book in this way, we may give away the introduction for free and charge for the remainder of the book. Or we could give a summary version of the book away but charge for the full edition with the stories, examples and exercises that bring it to life.

Q. Now reimagine your business as if it operates as a marketplace for others in your industry to buy and sell from one another. You don't own any assets, products or services and act as a facilitator, like eBay or Airbnb.

A. If we reimagined this book as a marketplace, we wouldn't even write the book, and instead we'd operate a platform to aggregate great content from other people in the entrepreneurial community. As the community grows, we may charge a small transactional fee for those trading through the marketplace.

Q. Next, reimagine your business as if you sell one large up-front purchase that ties your customers to you for future purchases of ancillary products, like printers and cartridges or razors and blades.

A. This book might look more like an online course where you pay up front for an initial period, let's say 12 weeks, and then additional or updated modules come at an additional price.

Q. Lastly, reimagine your business as if customers sign up to purchase from you on a subscription basis rather than a single one-off purchase.

A. If this book were a subscription, we could break each chapter down into a weekly or monthly course or challenge and readers could receive it episodically, giving them time to actively work through the exercises.

I could do this all day…

This is one of my absolute favourite exercises to do and by now you should have at least four different options for how you could operate your business should a major crisis impact the way you currently do business. As well as a number of ideas for where you could take the business next. Even just writing that has given me a whole host of ideas for Misadventures in Entrepreneuring already, so watch this space!

Try even more options with different business models like McDonald's, Ryanair, insurance companies, gym memberships, Amazon or Costco.

This kind of exercise really paid dividends for us at Entrepreneurial Spark when we operated 12 physical accelerator hubs across all the major cities in the UK, but really lacked a presence in rural areas. It simply wasn't feasible to have a physical space and ask people to travel hundreds of miles, or in some cases from different islands, to benefit from the programme. We had to reimagine it, and our virtual accelerator model was born.

Shortly afterwards, we delivered two pilot virtual accelerator programmes in rural areas of the UK and the virtual model now forms the backbone of the business that Entrepreneurial Spark continues to deliver to entrepreneurs, corporate and local government customers.

Try to practise applying this in situations where you don't feel under pressure emotionally, or where the future of the business isn't resting on the outcome and you'll find that when it really matters, situations won't feel quite so black and white.

Try to combine all three of these mental training techniques:

- Taking the time to learn and reflect from previous misadventures.
- Carving out time to develop yourself and build your mental strength.
- Practise your ability to reimagine daily.

If you can do this, then I promise that the day a real obstacle arises, and it will, it's going to look different. It may even look like an opportunity to you and wouldn't that be nice?

If you can't do this for yourself then get enabled

The last thing to note is that all of this mental training is not an easy thing to do by yourself. Holding up the mirror and doing some deep and reflective work on yourself is tough to do alone. If you find that you can't get yourself unstuck, then find someone to help – like the time we brought the coach in to help us with our new leadership dynamic and our external relationships.

Lucy-Rose is a accredited coach and I used to think that was a really pink and fluffy thing reserved for people who were looking to discover themselves – who knew I was one of those people! And so, it turns out that coaching is in fact cool. And it's not therapy, although sometimes I wish it was.

At Entrepreneurial Spark our entire business model was built on the foundation that entrepreneurs didn't need any more of the freely available advice on how to run a business: they needed coaching, enablement and accountability to become better entrepreneurs.

So we recruited, trained and managed a team of 26 entrepreneurial enablers (similar to coaches) who worked one-to-one with entrepreneurs to hold up the mirror to their behaviour, ask those carefully crafted questions, hold their hand when they needed it and kick their butt when they needed that too. With regular one-to-ones as well as peer-to-peer accountability, this type of support meant entrepreneurs could take quick corrective action if they were going off course, and often went further and faster than they could ever have achieved had they been on their own.

If you are thinking that you are doing OK on your own and you don't need any of that, I'm sure you are, but consider this for a moment. In the six years we ran Entrepreneurial Spark, we enabled around 4,000 entrepreneurs, who in that time turned over £651 million in turnover, raised £255 million in investment, created 8,096 jobs and had an incredible 87% survival rate. I think we were doing something right!

You don't have to develop yourself as an entrepreneur; you don't have to work on your mindset, your self-awareness, your impact on yourself and others, your resilience and mental strength; and you don't have to get enabled… but imagine what could happen if you did?

If you've never been enabled then I challenge you to get a coach, even just for a session or two to see what difference it makes. Coaches are superhuman people who have high levels of emotional intelligence and their superpower is superhuman in helping you to see the wood from the trees if you're stuck with something.

They do it by asking carefully crafted and sometimes very wonderfully intuitive questions that force you to look at your situation from a different perspective. Find a coach that gets you, adds value without even asking. Don't just choose the first one you meet: speak to a few until you really feel that instant connection and then watch as a new version of you emerges to take on challenges and obstacles with a fresh perspective and a new sense of bravery.

Course correction questions

- When was the last time you set aside time to work on you?
- How are you going to carve out more time to do that?
- If you're struggling to do this on your own, how could you identify the right critical friend or coach to support you?

What do you need to... Stop, Start and Continue doing now?

STOP

- Assuming you can become better, stronger or more resilient without putting in the work

- Thinking you can do everything and make changes alone

START

- Building in time to work on yourself – schedule time with yourself like you would with other people

- Doing mental workouts as well as physical ones – diarize this

- Looking for a coach, an accountability buddy, a healthcare professional or anyone else that can help hold a mirror up to you, can hold you accountable to keep making progress and can support and encourage you to keep going when things feel tough

---

CONTINUE

- Building that resilience muscle with regular exercise and brain food

- Your self-awareness adventure, learning more about the fantastic being that you are so that you can continue to grow in new unchartered territory beyond any of your previous expectations for yourself

Bonus exercise: Schedule yourself a mental workout

Your bonus exercise for this chapter is to schedule that mental workout with yourself and stick to it. I'd like you to think of that thing that you would love to do but have been putting off for months or 'just haven't got round to it' because you believe that you are too busy or other things are more important. I have news. Nothing is more important than becoming a better version of your entrepreneurial self – just think what you're going to be able to achieve then.

So here goes.

1. Open up your diary and pick a time – preferably one where you know that interruptions will be at a minimum. You're going to make sure that you won't be disturbed but it will lessen the guilt at being off the grid for an hour.
2. Schedule a meeting in the next seven days with yourself.
3. If other people have control of your calendar, then make sure this time is set to do not disturb.
4. At the time of the meeting, go somewhere that isn't somewhere you would regularly work. Make it somewhere comfortable, or somewhere you might be anonymous. (I like to go to the business room at the gym; that way it feels

just like going to the gym and in my head, I'm working out!) Whatever works for you though. Why not try a new coffee shop and treat yourself to a nice coffee or a hot chocolate?

5. This goes without saying but please put your phone on 'do not disturb' and if you're using a tablet or device shut down your emails.

6. Pull out your *Misadventures in Entrepreneuring Journal* and pick that one thing you've been putting off for this very moment and get to work. Challenge yourself, practise scenario planning, reflect on a previous misadventure and your learnings, read up about thinking errors! There are so many valuable things you could be doing right now that will build your confidence and your ability to entrepreneur every day.

7. Fight the urge to look at your phone after five minutes. I promise you all of the things you think you are needed for right now are only in your head.

8. Enjoy yourself!

9. Get another coffee if you feel the urge.

10. At the end of the time you've allowed yourself, you can stop and return to all of the things that you thought were way more important than that, knowing that you have just improved your ability to deal with them.

Now that you've done that ask yourself:

- How did it feel? Did you enjoy it or were you worried?
- If you were worried, did any of the things you were worried about materialize?
- Did you have enough time to complete your task?
- When are you going to schedule the next self-development session in? Is it going to become a regular session alongside your weekly yoga or game of five-a-side football?
- What are you going to tackle next?

After I did this the first time, I was so energized that I couldn't wait to do it again. And then life got in the way and I cheated on myself with what I believed was 'other more important work'. It takes time to build the habit so scheduling these in regularly is a good way to make sure you keep it up.

9

Misadventures in...

KNOWING WHEN YOU'VE REACHED
THE END

When we first began research for this book, the intention was to write about our experiences of misadventuring as entrepreneurs and what that felt like. And while that is what the book has been about up until this point, as we get to the end it feels as though we should also really talk about the potential for life after this particular chapter of entrepreneuring. Who writes about that? Who tells you when to move on? Or how it will feel? And what on earth happens next?

At the time of writing this book, Lucy-Rose and I have made two profound decisions in our life together as entrepreneurs. The first was to exit from Entrepreneurial Spark, and the second was not to carry on with Misadventures in Entrepreneuring in the format we first envisaged. It feels fitting that as we get to the end of writing a book about how to navigate your way through life as an entrepreneur, we conclude it by ending this particular part of our own adventure and then telling you about our experience of it not just once, but twice.

This chapter is about exploring the idea that reaching the end is a possibility and being in control of how and when rather than being blindsided by it. In this final chapter, we'll explore the difference between temporary and permanent feelings, when you'll know you need to make a change and how it's going to feel when you do.

Nothing lasts forever

I was discussing this chapter with my writing coach, and she asked me: 'Does thinking about the end before you start influence the way you set up your business in the beginning?' It's a really interesting question and I believe there are a couple of ways to look at this.

Most people will tell you that when you set up it's good to think about the structure of the business and what happens should things not go right. If you have a business partner and you fall out and one wants to leave, does the shareholding matter? If you haven't registered as a limited company, then what happens if you go bust and you have outstanding debt like a three-year lease on a premises in your own name? Who is liable?

These and about a zillion others are all really good questions to ask yourself in the beginning… as long as you don't spend too long dwelling on the 'what if' scenarios. Any or all of those things could and might happen and you can safeguard for some but not the others. The important thing is to not be too afraid of what might happen that you end up doing nothing! That *is* a sure-fire way to make sure your business ends before it even gets off the ground. Balance is the aim of the game here.

What I've come to realize is that what is just as important as safeguarding yourself legally in the beginning is to have an understanding of the kind of circumstances or conditions that would leave you firmly in control of a decision to call it a day. This doesn't mean that you enter into business assuming or willing it to end. It's more like being aware that nothing lasts forever and scenario planning so that you don't wake up one morning and wonder how you ended up continuing past a point that it doesn't make sense any more only to be surprised at how on earth you got there.

It's about being aware of what does and doesn't work for you and being able to be in control of how and when you make a decision to quit.

Having made the decision to quit twice, I can safely say that we did not do this first time around. With Entrepreneurial Spark, Lucy-Rose and original co-founder Jim Duffy focused their attention on the likely contractual scenarios the business might encounter in partnering with a large corporate and built safeguards into our contract that meant that legally the business was protected in the event the partnership ended.

When I took over from Jim as a director, it was a given that we had that funding and there didn't seem to be any need to have a conversation that asked at what point does this not work for us any more. We had a five-year rolling contract with one of the largest commercial banks in the world for a lot of funding. It almost seemed ridiculous to even think that we would instigate an end. Let me reiterate – we had funding for five years for a team of over 40 people and 12 locations nationally, at any point in time, renewed every year if we kept meeting milestones – what's not to like?

Until we actually did wake up one day and realize we'd *almost* continued past a point that it didn't make sense any more. It wasn't that anything was wrong per se: we had funding, we'd built an amazing team, the model worked, we were oversubscribed in terms of customers, and our year-on-year impact report was increasingly impressive. Yet if you looked closely, some gaps had begun to appear that on the surface seemed small but in reality became fundamental deal-breakers.

We'd reached a stage where we were debating which brand represented what we were trying to do – we realized it was neither. We weren't a bank initiative, or a start-up; we were a kind of hybrid. What was our strength in the beginning had become confusing for the customer, and we'd somewhat lost our identity.

We had also recruited, trained and grown a phenomenal team, but with such a flat structure that the opportunities for progression within our current model were limited. We knew any one of them would be an asset to any organization and we wanted to create as many opportunities for them to thrive as we could. We knew something had to change.

We started asking hard questions of ourselves and explored the seemingly inconceivable idea that we could and should end the partnership. I still have the notebook with the words 'go nuclear option' circled in permanent marker. That was two years ago and look at what's changed. It's hard to believe that considering that we should end it all could have felt like the end of the world.

Second time around, we've grown up. Hard questions are second nature, and the notion that things can end feels much less personal. Of course, we don't have 40 staff to consider this time around, which was the toughest and most emotionally taxing consideration for us last time, so the decision feels less dramatic from that perspective, but no less dramatic on our own individual lives.

Are these feelings temporary?

To go back to the initial question from my coach about doing things differently if you had the end in mind, I believe that there is a degree of planning you can do. But things change so markedly along the journey that you can never really plan for the end until you know it's happening. And the only way to know it's happening is to be self-aware, interpret your feelings and determine if you've hit a deal-breaker.

The thing that determining your deal-breakers up front and being in control of the decision-making process helps you to do is figure out if what you're feeling on a day-to-day basis is temporary or if it's settled in for the long haul. Can you get over it, move on and still make a success of this business? Or has a seed of doubt been sown in your gut and it's time for you to take more notice that you're approaching a deal-breaker?

What we didn't realize at the time with Entrepreneurial Spark, which we now know in hindsight, is that Lucy-Rose and I had established some subconscious unspoken deal-breakers that we weren't even aware of. It wasn't until we got some help to rationalize why we felt this wasn't working that we realized we'd crossed some of them. I bet you have some that you're not even conscious of too.

For us it felt like:

- We've outgrown our original plans, and this doesn't fit with our new direction.
- We're compromising our values too often.
- This doesn't feel like it's us any more.

We could have coped with adjusting our plans and goals if we were still working towards the same vision, and we did so multiple times. We would have been happy to compromise on one or two values if we were convinced it was going to help us to achieve our goal of supporting entrepreneurs more rapidly or effectively.

We loved feeling like the odd couple of a start-up and a corporate working perfectly side by side to do something bigger than either could achieve on their own, and we were happy to adopt more corporate practices to make this partnership work even better.

What worried us, was losing the magic of what made them want to partner with us in the first place and that was being able to think and act like a start-up. And we were beginning not to recognize ourselves.

We didn't know we were going to exit in the beginning but once the seed had been planted about what was possible 'on the other side', it was almost impossible to think about doing it any other way. When we started to believe that our job was done, and we needed a new mission, we knew it was time for someone else to continue our legacy.

Everyone will be different when it comes to the things that drive us to make a change. What motivated us won't necessarily be true for you despite my confidence that all of those statements will probably resonate with you.

The difference for us was that these feelings started off as temporary and then became permanent.

If you've never thought about a controlled decision to end your relationship with your business where you are proactive then give it a try. You might find you are exactly where you want to be. And you might also find that some of the temporary hard feelings we've talked about in Chapters 1–8 so far are starting to become permanent – this is not a misadventure – this might be a good time to make a change. And that's OK.

Either way, I promise it's not as scary as you might think. What's scarier is staying where you are if it isn't working for you.

If you want to try it out, then begin by thinking about a set of circumstances that you definitely don't want for yourself. This is a technique I use when I find the list of things that I do want to be infinite and the choice is too overwhelming and not very helpful. I find it easier to start with the things I definitely don't want and work back from there.

They might look something like:

- I don't want to feel like I'm missing out on other opportunities.
- I don't want to feel bored or fed up every day.
- I don't want to feel like this is just too hard.
- I don't want to feel like I'm stuck in the past or I don't fit the skin I'm in.
- I don't want to compromise.
- I don't want to settle.
- I don't want to do this any more.

Now, let's face it: you've made it this far and these are completely normal things to feel some of the time. The monumental task that you have taken on is breathtaking and the personal growth journey incredible. You've learned that it's OK to be winging it and you're getting the hang of it. You've learned to overcome feelings that you don't have what it takes, or other people are better or more experienced than you. Then came the realization that this entrepreneuring thing isn't the work/life balance you thought it was and in fact eating, sleeping and breathing our businesses was going to be harder work than we've ever done. Then came the people, those beautiful employees with their amazing talents... accompanied by all of their HR needs. And let's not forget the assh*les.

And, of course, you have spent years bringing everyone else along on the journey with you – customers, suppliers, funders, not to mention your family who are all very proud of your efforts but still think you're batsh*t crazy and you should go and get a *real job*. And maybe you found a new relationship, ended an old one, had a family, had the family grow up and leave, moved to a new house, moved to a new country or experienced some other life-altering event!

It's really no wonder you're no stranger to some of those feelings. Congratulations – what a ride! Now take a breath and tell me this: have they settled in or will it pass like it has many times before? Take a look at the feelings again and build on them:

- I don't want to feel bored or fed up every day. Some days I'm going to have to do things that I don't like doing, so when things feel like drudgery over and over again – what needs to change?
- I don't want to feel downhearted all the time. I have a stack of resilience and mental toughness and I know days are going to feel hard so when this feels like more pain than it's worth – what needs to change?
- I don't want to feel like I'm missing out on other opportunities. I know that I can't hop from one opportunity to the next like a magpie so when I feel constantly like I'm being held back – what needs to change?
- I don't want to feel like I'm stuck in the past or I don't fit the skin I'm in any more. I know that I set myself a vision and it's normal to evolve along the way, so when I feel as though I don't recognize myself in that vision any longer – what needs to change?
- I don't want to compromise. I recognize that entrepreneuring is going to be full of trade-offs and I'll have to choose what gives on a daily basis, so when I feel as though everything is a compromise and there is only give and no take – what needs to change?

- I don't want to settle. I know that life isn't a bed of roses all of the time and some days will be up and some will be down, so when I feel as though I deserve to be happier, or more valued, or more worthy – what needs to change?
- I don't want to do this any more. I know that the magic happens outside of my comfort zone and I know all the theory about the moment you want to stop is usually right before something great is about to happen, so when the feeling of being exhausted and wanting to stop continues past a temporary pain barrier – what needs to change?

If the answer is 'nothing at the moment', crack on. The feeling was temporary, you were having a bad day, or week, or even a month but you've pushed past it and the desire to carry on still far outweighs the desire to stop.

If doing this exercise has struck a chord, then it may be time to dig a bit deeper. Go on and ask yourself some more probing questions and see if you can get to the bottom of the feeling. If you're fearful of doing it on your own, then try out loud (yes, out loud is even more terrifying) and with someone else (who won't let you off the hook). The rule of the game is that you have to be deadly honest: no excuses, denial or pretend BS. And then brace yourself to learn how you really feel because the answers might not be what you expect.

(Tip – don't try this with friends and family, only a supporter or critical friend. You're much more likely to be honest and it's less likely they will try to influence you.)

Try these:

- *Why are you tired/fed up/bored/missing out/compromising etc.?* – Good warm-up question.

- *What could you do to change this feeling?* – Again, a nice simple one with lots of follow-ups like 'If you were to change one thing about your day then what would it be?'
- *What is it about doing this that has changed to make you feel this way now that you didn't before?* – There may be bits of what you're doing that you really don't like, true story. Lucy-Rose and I believed that you could only be successful if you could scale your business – so we did. Then we realized that a scale business wasn't the be all and end all. We missed the human interaction, the connection and the agility of a smaller business. Careful what you wish for.
- *What would invigorate you again?* – What seems like another nice easy one may surprise you. What would you rather be doing and how would it feel if you were doing it? Go on, spit it out. This is the time for thinking about the things you do want, now you've got the 'don't wants' out of the way. Like the realization of not wanting a scale business meant being more in control, connecting at a more human-to-human level and getting back to working one-to-one or one-to-few with people again.

Doing what is right for you, not what is necessarily easy, can feel hugely uncomfortable at the time, but you will thank yourself in the long run. But, can you trust that doing what is right *will* come as a relief and *will* ultimately feel easier?

When we created Misadventures in Entrepreneuring we believed, and still do, that we had a duty to tell our story and the stories of others so that everyone could benefit. We didn't know how but we just knew that it was the right moment to invest our time and our resources into whatever the eventual outcome was going to be. We began by documenting our own story and by interviewing other entrepreneurs over the course of a year to collect their stories too.

As it turned out, we met some incredible people who told some hugely brave and emotional stories about struggles and successes and we knew that we had done something powerful by unlocking these. By complete fluke we recorded all of these by audio and video, so that I could go back and listen and draw out relevant anecdotes that would fit with each chapter of this book.

After a while, light dawned that we actually had some really useful content that we could get to the people that needed it by different mediums, and much quicker (and less painfully) than writing a book – so we launched the Misadventures in Entrepreneuring Podcast.

Neither of us had any experience in writing, publishing, recording, creating podcasts, launching and promoting podcasts, social media campaigns, building websites and building email mailing lists, or any of the other technical skills required to make this anything other than a project that we really enjoyed undertaking – we just wanted to talk to interesting people and tell interesting and helpful stories.

This is our passion project and we've loved every minute of it, but as we know from Chapter 3, passion does not pay the bills. As time went on, we knew that we were going to have to find a way to make our passion project sustainable if we wanted to carry on. Although we looked at different models we couldn't find quite the right one at that time.

The truth was that although this gave us so much joy, we were also finding it pretty tough. The technical skill side of the business was hard for both of us. I love learning new creative skills but as a beginner it took so long and was really inefficient.

The perfectionist in me wasn't allowing myself to 'just get stuff out there' in a really rough and ready way and get feedback. I found I was putting myself under pressure to create something polished before anyone saw it.

As I write this, I know it is something I have to work on for every project that I embark on in the future because it can eat away at your brain and prevent you from enjoying what you're doing in the pursuit of trying to make things perfect.

For Lucy-Rose, the creative technical skill side of the business just wasn't something she enjoys doing. She thrives in human contact and in an environment where she can really get stuck in and make a difference, seeing a big picture that others rarely see and moving around the component parts to make it all work like a well-oiled machine (a tight ship as her mother used to refer to it) and this just wasn't it.

We found every day a bit of a slog. It was affecting our relationship as we struggled to search for a business model that could make this work for us, knowing all the while that the model we knew that could be an option was one that involved us doing things that Lucy-Rose didn't enjoy and I was going to become a frustrated slow learner. Something had to give. In the end, we hit the pause button in that moment to put our relationship before a business that we hadn't even created yet because we already knew that those feelings would not be temporary if we carried on down this road. We knew we needed time to go back to the drawing board and figure out what we really wanted as individuals and where we wanted to invest our precious time.

Roz Hutchings – Disco Dance Bristol

When I left my salaried position, I remember vividly how elated, light and buoyant I felt. I walked down the road and I'd booked into my favourite yoga class, which was a real treat. I actually skipped down the road with a sense of uplifting relief. I knew that from this minute on everything I do is on my terms, every penny I make will be mine; I won't be frustrated about feeling undervalued or disrespected. I could make anything happen; it was such an open horizon!

Year one was great: we brought on a big client and it was a bit dreamy. This is cool; this is amazing… until the retainer was pulled. I hadn't even thought it could be pulled so quickly so I wasn't prepared. I'll get something else and it will sort itself out, I thought, and ever since then it's been an uphill slog. Constant thoughts of money, bills being paid, balancing that out with money coming in on time, chasing customers. Questioning do I deliver the work vs. pushing for more customers. Having that three-way debate with myself all the time.

The final straw was really off the back of people just not responding to proposals that I'd spent ages putting together. I've still got 30 proposals in my pipeline system with no answer. At the start of 2019 I started to meditate and listen to myself. Perhaps I was sending out vibes that I didn't really want all of those pipeline proposals approved – because then I've actually got to do it!

I started to learn, listen and understand all that. So, if not this, what would be next, what is the thing you really want to do…? You have the confidence to go back to your truest self in meditation and stop all the other conversations in my head getting in the way. Music and dance were what appeared; it's what I've always done so why can't I make a business out of that? My close circle had mixed opinions but I thought sod it I can do this – so I am.

As we've already talked about, great entrepreneurs are constantly curious about themselves and the world around them. So if you're checking in with yourself on a regular basis, then it shouldn't come as a surprise when the end comes into view. At least that's the theory anyway.

Exiting, failure and fear

Exiting and failure are two of the most overused and misunderstood words in start-up lexicon that highly misrepresent the way that most entrepreneurs truly move on from their businesses.

The great and mythical 'exit' has become somewhat of a holy grail in start-up land, like the unicorn. After all, what could be cooler than becoming an entrepreneur, building a start-up, raising investment, scaling, then exiting? Lots of things, actually, we've discovered. Business can be great, and cool, and worthy, and impactful without becoming any of these things, and without an investor banging a door down to offer you a seven-figure swansong.

The word 'exit', or the notion of 'getting to an exit', has got a lot to answer for when it comes to misguidedness, or ego, pushing entrepreneurs to continue past a point of logical sense to step away. This can also cause you to *be exited*, which is something far less pleasant.

Failure also has a lot to answer for, or at least societal conditioning around failure, as well as its use in start-up vocabulary. There has been a huge push from the start-up community in the last 10 years to reframe the word 'failure'. To make it less final or less scary; to encourage us to fail regularly to build our resilience and tenacity in the face of adversity. At Entrepreneurial Spark we talked a lot about failing fast, smart and cheap by way of demonstrating to entrepreneurs that it was OK to try, and if it didn't work out that was OK too.

In hindsight, I think we chose the wrong word, or at least became part of the conditioning problem. By talking about failure all the time, despite the effort to reframe the word 'failure', society still tells us that if we are failing, we are not succeeding, or worse, we are failures.

Having observed thousands of entrepreneurs in our accelerator over the years, more often than not it's this relationship that we have with failure that in turn creates fear. And then ultimately, it's the *fear* that prevents us from being really honest with ourselves and staying in situations way longer than we should.

We've talked quite a lot about fear in the previous chapters and in my experience most misadventures come down to fear at some level.

> *What if I fall? Oh, but my darling, what if you fly?*
> Erin Hanson[22]

There is so much to be fearful of in entrepreneuring, and if we let it, it could stop us from ever beginning, which is an end in itself. Yet it's the boldness to overcome the fear that becomes an opportunity that we could never imagine.

If you have been so bold up until this point, it would be criminal to let a fear of failure get you now. Ask yourself: if the feelings are permanent, why am I still doing what I'm doing? Is

---

[22] Erin Hanson (2014), *Voyage (The Poetic Underground #2)*, www.lulu.com/en/gb/shop/erin-hanson/voyage-the-poetic-underground-2/paperback/product-1zkdj5ng.html.

it because I really want to, and I see an opportunity too good to give up on? Or is it because I'm scared to believe that I look like a failure, or I am a failure?

On the flip side, it would be criminal to let a different kind of fear get you now, to make you give up before you have reached your potential – the fear of success. This comes as a surprise to a lot of people that someone might self-sabotage because they are going to be successful and not the other way around. For some though, this can be a very real thing and those temporary feelings we described previously might just be a resistance to change. And I *know* by now that you've got your head around the fact that you are living in a world of change (and if you haven't, go back to Chapter 7).

Exiting isn't the cool and sexy thing that Silicon Valley has made it out to be, and failure (and success) isn't something to be fearful of. All either of them really means is just another change: the closing of one door and the opening of another.

Lucy-Rose was the brave one in Misadventures in Entrepreneuring who put her hand up and said she thought it was time she looked at what she really wanted to be doing, something to really fulfil her and make her feel more like herself again. It was such a courageous move, knowing all of the history that we have together and the deep desire within us both to create something together, to then call time.

It's also something I would have been slower to come around to because of my dogged determination to see something through to conclusion, even if I already know it isn't working. That was my fear of failure kicking in. None of us are immune.

What's important is to take the time to check in with yourself and recognize if what you're feeling is a temporary state or if it has moved in permanently. Take the time to play with the possibilities using the same hard questioning techniques we talked about earlier in the chapter. And remember, you don't have to make any snap decision here; this is always about you being in control of where this ends up, and that's pretty powerful.

Let's not pretend that it isn't going to happen. Instead, focus on enjoying the ride while it lasts and get out before it changes so much you don't enjoy it any more. Then move on to the next great thing you will do, taking with you everything you have learned.

Post-exit feelings

If you do decide to make a change, I hope it has been the way you planned or hoped. I have seen entrepreneurs for whom the end has been a surprise and it's quite an emotional trauma to overcome.

In either circumstance, remember that you have given over your life, you've made sacrifices and you've made trade-offs for this business. You have gained and lost people in your life and you've shed at least one or two skins to grow into the person you are now. It stands to reason that once that isn't in your life any more, it will create a vacuum. I've heard it described by some as empty nest syndrome. Like everything, this is also OK.

For two months after we exited from Entrepreneurial Spark, I spent most of my time trapped in a cycle of:

- ✓ Being terrified at 'not having a job'
- ✓ Feeling elated to be able to go to the gym every morning
- ✓ Feeling guilty for not starting work promptly at 8am
- ✓ Desperately searching for a purpose

✓   Eagerly anticipating what's next

I also wrote the following diary entry for draft one of the book and then the second one for this final version…

3 May 2018

When Lucy-Rose and I exited the business, we were transferring 29 members of our team to another business and were so focused on how they felt that we didn't really have time to compile our own thoughts and feelings about it. When I was asked the only way I could describe it was to say that it felt like I imagine my mother felt the day she sent me off to university – sad that her baby no longer needs her, trepidation at what would become of me in the big bad world, and excited for my future, all mixed with a huge dose of pride at what we'd achieved together. And two months down the line I still feel the same. No regrets.

1 Jan 2020

And at the time of writing this, the future of Misadventures in Entrepreneuring is unknown – it always has been – and we wouldn't have it any other way. We're so hugely proud of how we've spent the last 18 months, of having the bravery and the audacity to think that we could write a book or launch a podcast and then actually going and doing it. We never knew where this would take us, but it's been a fantastic adventure and we feel so privileged to have met new people, learned new skills, grown enormously as humans, cemented another chapter in our lives and to come out of the end still with no regrets.

WHAT'S NEXT?

If you are thinking of making a change then rest assured that those post-exit feelings don't last for very long. I already trust that you have put into practice some of the suggestions from this book about preparing yourself for change and embracing the unknown. So when the time comes, I know that you are going to be ready for that rollercoaster.

Think of it like the time you made a hard decision to end a relationship in your life. You said an emotional goodbye to the ex and for a while nothing could compare. Until one day a new opportunity crossed your path and showed you how attractive it could be if you could only shake off those feelings of pining for the past.

Before you know it, you're off on a new exciting and totally unexpected adventure and you're going to go through all of the same thoughts and feelings as you've been through on the last one. And just think how much more you know about yourself and what you want from life.

Don't be afraid to take your time figuring out what you want from the next chapter, but equally don't be so worried that you won't get it right that you end up standing still. Remember that being a good or a great entrepreneur is about embracing the fact that you are (almost) always both the problem and the solution to becoming great. The same goes for your next phase.

What's next for us?

What's next for us? Good question. We're still working on figuring out that dastardly business model and trying to stay on the right side of turning our passion into a business.

Until then we're doing what comes naturally and working with entrepreneurs to cut through the fog when you need it and to always bring that human-first approach to entrepreneuring. As anxious worriers, we are the ideal people to call on in a crisis or when you think you're misadventuring – trust us, we've planned for this. We love nothing more than to unscramble you when you're stuck, help you to work out what feeling *less* guilty looks like, and be a champion for you when you're feeling alone. If you think you need some of that in your life, then we can work with you and your team.

We also have unrivalled experience at helping others who want to help entrepreneurs. If you're reading this and you're looking to support a group of entrepreneurs to go further and faster, then let us help. We built the world's largest fully funded entrepreneurial accelerator and worked with over 4,000 entrepreneurs; we've seen all the pitfalls and we've had all the misadventures for you. As we live in a world where entrepreneurial skills are regarded as 21st-century skills and are being embraced by many, we can give you the guidance and support needed.

Find us at www.misadventuresinentrepreneuring.com/tribe for all the ways we can help.

And if you have read this book and there is something you need help with or have a story to tell, what I do know is that www.misadventuresinentrepreneuring.com/tribe will always be a sanctuary for honest conversation about the reality of being an entrepreneur.

What I also know is that some people you meet on this adventure will be with you for life. So, don't worry, Lucy-Rose and I will still be partners in crime – always supporting one another to take those tentative next steps to do something new and daring. And we'll be having many more misadventures and course correcting with one another as we go.

We hope you are too.

Course correction questions

- ◉ Why are you tired/fed up/compromising/bored/missing out etc.?
- ◉ What could you do to change this feeling?
- ◉ What is it about doing this that has changed to make you feel this way now that you didn't before?
- ◉ What would invigorate you again?

What do you need to... Stop, Start and Continue doing now?

- ◉ Only you can decide this time
